Metamorphosis

Metamorphosis

5 Steps to Releasing Trauma and Awakening Your True Self

Sydel Sierra

Copyright © Sydel Sierra 2023
First published by the kind press 2023

The moral right of the author to be identified as the author of this work has been asserted.

All rights reserved. Without limiting the rights under copyright reserved above, no part of this publication may be reproduced, stored in or introduced into a retrieval system, or transmitted, in any form or by any means (electronic, mechanical, photocopying, recording or otherwise) without the prior written permission of the publisher of this book.

A catalogue record for this book is available from the National Library of Australia.

Trade Paperback ISBN: 978-0-6458656-2-2
eBook ISBN: 978-0-6458656-1-5

Print information available on the last page.

We at The Kind Press acknowledge that Aboriginal and Torres Strait Islander peoples are the Traditional Custodians and the first storytellers of the lands on which we live and work; and we pay our respects to Elders past and present.

THE
KIND
PRESS

www.thekindpress.com

This book deals with sexual abuse, traumatic or triggering themes. While the author has taken great lengths to ensure the subject matter is dealt with in a compassionate and respectful manner, it may be troubling for some readers. Discretion is advised. All of the events are true to the best of the author's memory. Some names and identifying features have been changed to protect the identity of certain parties. The views expressed in this book are solely those of the author. We advise that the information contained in this book does not negate personal responsibility on the part of the reader for their own health and safety. It is sold with the understanding that the author and publisher are not engaged in rendering advice or any other kind of personal or professional service in the book. In the event that you use any of the information in this book for yourself, the author and the publisher assume no responsibility for your actions.

Contents

A Note On Trust	viii
Introduction	x
Who Is This Book For?	xii
Why I Wrote This Book	xiv
Everyone Deserves To Heal	xvii

Part One My Story — 1

The Day I Met My Abuser	3
A Very Bad Path	4
Under His Spell	7
Who Are The Elite?	9
Altered States	12
On The Inside	14
The Escape	16

Part Two My Healing — 19

Wave 1: Facing The Reality Of Your Past	23
Wave 2: Navigating The Rollercoaster Of Healing	51
Wave 3: Positive Shifts, Empowerment And Self-Worth	97
Wave 4: Becoming Present And Leaving The Past	127
Wave 5: Claiming Your Life Back	157

Appendix: Healing Modalities	177
To Those Who Helped	187
About The Author	189

A Note On Trust

Before I share my story, I want to first talk about the concept of trust. It's fundamental to any functional society and underpins many of the structures we rely upon today. In fact, we cannot build healthy relationships, communities or operate as a civilisation if we don't have it.

Think about this for a moment. We trust that:
- Money will appear in our bank account when promised
- Our financial systems will safeguard our money responsibly
- The food we buy is fresh and suitable for eating
- Our neighbours will act in good faith toward us
- Our friends and family can be relied upon for loyalty and support
- Our legal system can be counted on to provide just and fair outcomes

These are just a few examples, but the more we think about it, the more apparent it is that trust is the glue that holds society together. By default, we tend to be more trusting than suspicious of one another because we simply couldn't function any other way. To live without trust is to live in fear, and if we're suspicious of everyone around us, our world would be a very scary place.

However, to live with trust is incredibly beautiful and freeing. When trust remains intact, it has a positive effect on relationships, communities and societies. When it's maintained consistently over time, it deepens to a whole new level.

But trust can also be weaponised and abused. And in the hands of someone skilled enough, it can be used to manipulate, deceive, exploit and harm—with devastating consequences. This explains how someone like me can fall prey to a dangerous, violent and abusive paedophile. It all happened right under the nose of my loving family. He took his time, he won the trust of everyone around me, and he eventually achieved his goal. He took me into the belly of an organised crime cult involved with trafficking, drugs, child abuse and murder.

Introduction

As a young child growing up in a middle-class Australian family, I was surrounded by people who loved and cared about me. I was a happy, gregarious child and I could immerse myself in creative activities for hours on end. My early years were filled with joyful experiences and opportunities. At age eleven, someone entered my life who irrevocably changed everything.

A paedophile.

By seventeen years of age, I was deep in the seedy underbelly of an organised crime cult, being abused on a regular basis. Drugged, tortured, experimented on and used for my special gifts, nobody in my life had a clue it was happening. Without going into the details of what I witnessed and experienced, I can say it involved drugs, child abuse, severe violence and the most horrific sexual and physical abuse. If I wasn't forced to participate, I was made to watch every excruciating detail of it first-hand. I endured countless and prolonged torture sessions where I was convinced I was going to die. My life was one big blur of painful experiences and no words will ever describe the unimaginable evil I was made to witness. And the worst

INTRODUCTION

part? I'd been groomed for years to accept it *all* as normal.

I eventually escaped my living hell, only to plunge headlong into a ten-year period of dissociative living. I had many toxic relationships and friendships during this time because I struggled to understand who I was. I struggled to accept love. I internalised a decade of mental and physical trauma while attempting to function as a normal person in the world. And I was processing my trauma and past alone, with not a single soul aware of what I'd been through—and survived. I lived this way for ten years until I reached the age of thirty and something remarkable happened. And that was the greatest gift of my life—***my healing.***

Who Is This Book For?

This book is for survivors of abuse, people living with trauma and anyone on a path of healing and self-discovery. We all have trauma to some degree, stubborn patterns that resurface and impact our lives and blockages we just can't seem to move past. Perhaps you've done self-development or inner work before, but still find yourself overwhelmed, insecure, in toxic relationships and asking yourself:

What's wrong with me?
I know I certainly did.

So, I went on a journey inward and unlocked many deep-seated beliefs within my own psyche that I had to release. But it wasn't just about releasing. It was about discovering things I never actually knew I lost. My self-worth and sovereignty.

Like so many people, I believed I wasn't worthy of help or of taking up space. If you feel like this, I encourage you to challenge these beliefs and let them go. Because the people who help you on your healing journey also get rewarded. They witness your full transformation and metamorphosis.

INTRODUCTION

Choose your own modality

One of the biggest discoveries I made when healing is that there wasn't *one* thing that did everything, but *every* thing changed one thing. Each puzzle piece on this journey helped create a complete picture of healing, and I used many different modalities to help me along the way, including traditional counselling, kinesiology, plant medicines, craniosacral therapy, remote healing and meditation (refer to Appendix A for the full list). I read books, talked to therapists and even talked to trusted friends who could handle the truth of my situation. I encourage you to combine this book with the healing modalities you intuitively resonate with to help you unlock and release. Different pathways will appeal to you at different stages, so use your discernment to gauge what's right for you.

Within these pages, I aim to give you the hope, encouragement and drive to go the whole way for yourself and integrate new and healthy patterns into your life. I hope this book illuminates your journey of self-inquiry and helps you create the life of your dreams.

Why I Wrote This Book

When I was going through my healing crisis, I felt alone, confused, and completely overwhelmed. I thought everything I was experiencing was in isolation and to be honest, it was terrifying. At times I wondered what was worse, the actual abuse or trying to heal from it years later.

My point is this:
I would have loved to have known that I wasn't alone.

This is the book I wish I had access to when I was navigating that metamorphic journey. It's a collection of some of my most challenging moments and how I overcame them, with insights and wisdom from my experiences before, during and after my healing crisis. Many times, I could have pulled the plug on the whole thing, but each time I managed to drag myself out of the metaphorical swamp and continue on.

However, this book is not just about the healing journey, it's about what you can find on the other side. Once I committed to healing the deeply broken and wounded parts of myself, something amazing happened. Slowly

INTRODUCTION

but surely, it got easier. Amidst the violent resurfacing of memories were fleeting moments of peace. Over time, the turbulence receded from my life. I regained control. I began to disintegrate every false belief I held about relationships and life. I worked hard to release my attachment to my trauma story and tap into my sovereignty and power instead. I had desired a normal life for so long, and I began to see it was not only possible, but well within my reach.

Everything started to change.

I met inspirational and positive people who wanted to uplift me, rather than suppress and drag me down. I experienced ease and alignment in my life and was drawn to new activities, projects and opportunities. For the first time in my life, I felt like I was actually living, rather than just 'coping and dealing'. As I continued to heal myself by rethinking and releasing my trauma, I found joy, happiness and abundance in every avenue of life—including love.

I've documented my journey and offer it to you in five stages—see them as waves—as they naturally move from one to the other.

Wave 1
Facing the reality of what happened and being truthful with yourself.

Wave 2
Purging the past and how the body gets 'rid' of trapped pain.

Wave 3
Reclaiming your greatest superpower, self-worth.

Wave 4
Becoming present and leaving your
traumatic past behind for good.

Wave 5
Creating an unimaginable life where
anything is possible.

This has been the most powerful, liberating, mind-blowing experience of my life and I promise you, when managed with intention, it will be the same for you, too. As you peel back each layer of your past pain, you'll uncover more strength, more wisdom, more compassion and more of your own gifts. You'll discover what you can leave behind and what you need to reclaim for yourself. It's all there for the taking and it will be the greatest gift you ever give yourself.

Why am I so sure of this?
Because in taking this opportunity, you'll experience something many people never do:

A complete metamorphosis and an awakening to who you truly are.

INTRODUCTION

Everyone Deserves To Heal

No single person on this earth is undeserving, unworthy or incapable of healing from their trauma and pain. That's simply a belief held by the wounded aspects of our minds. Trust me, if I can heal from everything that happened to me, so can you.

Every single one of us is influenced by our past, but if we never bring awareness and intention to what needs to be healed, we're not only living in avoidance, we're denying ourselves the chance to experience life beyond what we've been living. We're acquiescing to our traumatic past, rather than experiencing the richness of a fully integrated life.

I used to think my trauma was just a horrible misfortune and that all I could do was *hope for the best* based on what happened to me. I had no idea my wounded self was running the show, or that I was deeply limiting myself and living in a prison of my own making.

But here's the thing.
I held the key to escape.

METAMORPHOSIS

Beginning this journey is like coming to a fork in the road. One path looks familiar, but it leads you straight back to where you've always been, coping with life. This can look like fear, suffering, pain, detachment, avoidance, anxiety, depression and rage. The other path is unknown, but it offers rewards greater than anything you can imagine. If you take this path, you learn how to rethink your trauma, release it once and for all, and create a new reality that is fully aligned to who you are. This path takes commitment, and it isn't always easy, but it is worth it.

So, when I say you've come to your fork in the road, I offer you a choice:
- Will you allow your trauma to suppress you and control you for the rest of your life, or are you ready to meet the real you?
- What kind of life do you want?
- Are you ready to go the whole way and remember who you really are?

It took years for me to understand the reality of what I was part of. That realisation was the catalyst for a decade-long battle with PTSD and an intense, two-year healing journey where I released every layer of my trauma and battled every one of my demons.

I won.
And so can you.
Here is my story.

PART ONE
My Story

The Day I Met My Abuser

In the summer of the year 2000, I returned home from school to hear an unfamiliar voice inside the house. I pushed open the door to find a man sitting at our dining room table, engaged in conversation with my brother. I'd never seen him before, but my attention was immediately drawn to his appearance. He had long hair and wore skinny jeans with a collared shirt and blazer. He looked confident. When he caught sight of me, he swivelled his chair so he was looking at me dead in the eyes. He said, 'Hey man, your sister's pretty hot.'

I was an eleven-year-old in school uniform. This is how I met a stranger who would abuse me for the next decade of my life.

Whenever he was at our house, he made a point of acknowledging me, taking a genuine interest in my life and asking about my hobbies and schoolwork. In fact, he took notice of everything I was interested in and before long he'd created in-jokes between us to tease and make us laugh. He was at our house so often he became a regular fixture. A friend even.

The perfect base to begin building trust.

METAMORPHOSIS

A Very Bad Path

The person my family deeply trusted, with calculated precision, began to groom me. He engineered private moments and secret conversations between us, always finding more ways for us to be alone. Each encounter was deliberately shielded from my family. He was a master of making sure they were just out of earshot. When he had me alone, it was easy for him to plant seeds in my mind and create this false sense of intimacy between us, as though he was the only one who truly understood me. He'd carefully choose his words and statements to create distance between myself and my family, and closeness and trust between myself and him.

'You're special, aren't you?'
'You feel a lot more than you let on.'
'Your family doesn't really understand you.'
'You have special gifts, don't you?'

In a web of manipulation, he drew me closer and bound me to him in ever-increasing ways until I was convinced he could read my mind and see into my soul. I remember at one point feeling that he must be spying on me or listening to my conversations. I got so paranoid I started putting a blanket over my head at night so he couldn't read my mind.

PART ONE MY STORY

I'd switch off all the lights in my room because I thought he had a hidden camera somewhere filming me. I felt completely exposed and, to make it worse, I was dealing with this all on my own. He was unashamedly grooming me and nobody, not even me, knew it was happening.

It started with small and subtle touches. He'd covertly slide his hand up my leg while asking me, 'Are you okay with this?' It felt intrusive, uncomfortable and wrong, but I didn't know how to communicate that to an adult. I remember my eleven-year-old brain trying to rationalise the behaviour, thinking maybe *he does this with everyone?* I soon became convinced it was normal and I was simply overthinking.

I had no idea how to stop it.
So, it continued.

Before long, he was running his hands underneath my skirt. Each time he did, I became numb, felt trapped and frozen within a body that didn't feel like my own. Looking back, I understand that I was dissociating, my protective mechanisms kicking in to distance me from a situation I couldn't physically escape from. It wasn't long before the comments became sexualised, his questions more personal, and his touching more insistent and invasive. Bit by bit, year by year, he continued to break down my boundaries. They say most children in these situations never speak up about what they're experiencing. I was no different.

He gradually wore me down until my thoughts and feelings became a jumbled, confused mess. It's hard to explain just how complicated my relationship with him had become by this stage. On the one hand, I felt bullied and terrorised. On the other hand, I slowly became what he wanted me to be—helpless, malleable and stuck in the unfolding situation. A dangerous combination.

METAMORPHOSIS

When I became heavily dissociated to cope with what was happening, I learned that my responses to his questions often disappointed or angered him. So, I stopped responding in full sentences and used a nod or a nervous giggle instead. It was the safest thing to do. The combination of his inappropriate comments and manipulative tactics had a profound effect on me. It was disorienting, confusing and it meant one thing only.

I was being led down a very bad path.

PART ONE MY STORY

Under His Spell

I had just turned sixteen the first time he kissed me. I was so shocked I didn't know what to do. I said nothing. Later that evening, I called my best friend to tell her what had happened. My exact words were, 'If he thinks it's okay to kiss me, what is coming next?' I felt sick thinking about it.

He'd been grooming and manipulating me for five years by this stage. My family still trusted him implicitly, and I was so well groomed that I **gave *no* indication there *was*** anything to suspect. I was about to fall into an even darker and more sinister trap. The perfect foundation for abuse: trusted by family, easy access to me and pushing the boundaries with every single visit. Year by year, it all became normalised to the point where he could say or do anything to me, and I wouldn't blink an eye.

I was under his spell.

He began insisting that I travel to his house, rather than him coming to the family home. Here, we'd be perfectly isolated and far away from prying eyes. When I got my driver's licence, it opened up a world of opportunities for him to capitalise on. And so began the next level of abuse. Strategically, he took every opportunity to progress our twisted relationship. He constructed elaborate and violent fantasies that he'd whisper in my ear. He asked for photos of me as a child and teenager and photos of me wearing pretty dresses and make-up. He touched my legs, stroked my hair, caressed my skin and told me how perfect I was. He even took strands of my hair. I never found out why he wanted it or where it ended up. He kept pushing the physical boundaries until they became non-existent, and my response was always the same. Nod, smile, giggle.

As the physical abuse escalated, he also encouraged me to divulge personal information. He wanted to know every single thing about my life so there were no secrets between us. If I admitted I liked a boy, he'd call me a slut or a tease or a whore. Something as natural as liking a boy was seen as a malicious act of betrayal to him. I felt humiliated and ashamed of who I was for feeling things he disapproved of so violently. If I ever attempted to withhold information from him or change the story even slightly, he'd always know. His response would be instant and savage, 'I can spot when a bitch is lying to me.'

I gave up protecting what little privacy I had. I knew I had to answer truthfully or face being punished. I went along with whatever he wanted. He had access to my mind, my thoughts and my emotions. My body was next.

PART ONE MY STORY

Who Are The Elite?

Remember the first time he kissed me? Well, he told me that day it was all my fault because 'I cause men to react in crazy ways' and that 'I have a special energy no other woman has'. He was always doing this, reframing his acts to make me accountable for them.

Why didn't I ever ask for help?
The answer is simple. *I had no idea it was so wrong.*

My attitude and view of friendships, relationships and sex had been exclusively influenced by this time, and I felt like I existed solely under his rule. His warped ideas and views were so interwoven with my own, they were indistinguishable. Bit by bit, year by year, my self-expression became so limited that I was moulded into what he wanted me to be. The secret world with him felt closer than my lost reality.

Looking back, it's clear I was deeply intimidated and afraid. Why was I so fearful? Because of the terrifying things he told me. He dropped hints about what happened to people who broke the code of silence or didn't comply with orders. He described in detail the horrific tortures he'd watched people endure, all because they did not play ball. He described these people as 'worthless scum' or 'maggots' that deserved to die and be removed from the circle of elite and superior human beings. He had a theatrical storytelling manner and could go from yelling at the top of his voice to whispering inches from my face in a matter of seconds. He'd pound the table with his fists or stand up abruptly in the middle of a sentence. I'd sit quietly. Scared to move. Nodding my head. I never spoke up or went against his wishes for fear of the same thing happening to me. He was training me to distance myself from those types of people, reinforcing that I was different while communicating the type of behaviour he approved and disapproved of.

Pretty twisted, isn't it?
How. Did. It. Get. So Bad.

Once I turned seventeen, things drastically changed. His elaborate fantasies went from being about us to including other people, specifically, an elite group of people he deemed better than everyone else. He said that if I was worthy, I could join this group and play a very special role within it. I found myself thinking:

'I wonder if I'm special enough to be chosen?'
'What role would I play in this elite group?'
'Am I good enough to be accepted?'

According to him, my loyalty, intelligence and ability to listen and take instructions made me a perfect candidate. In other words, he knew I'd reached the required level of grooming and I was ready to be put to use. I was about to find out just how sinister these elites really were.

They are not elites at all. They're an organised crime cult involved in some of the most vile, dark and depraved activities you can imagine. I've wished so many times that I

PART ONE MY STORY

could go back and save my teenage self, just swoop her up and away from him and the hell he unleashed.

Altered States

I was about to enter the deepest, darkest hole I would ever fall down in my life—being introduced to the cult. This is where things got really bad.

Ketamine and a concoction of other drugs were added to my food and drinks to keep me in a deep state of confusion and incoherence. The dosages were calculated with precision and once they took hold, he would do whatever he pleased.

A note about altered states.
Much later in my years with the cult, I could identify the substances that were being used against me. It's common for people associated with cults to use hypnotics as an effective way to ensure complete control. In trauma studies, this form of abuse is also known as mind control.

While in this state, he planted subconscious beliefs into my mind so that in my waking or sober state, I would be easier to control. All of this was done through torture, and it lasted most of my seventeenth year. I endured a year of extreme sexual and psychological abuse until my cognitive function was overrun. I won't go into the specific details, but I'm sure you can guess the atrocities inflicted on a drugged and incoherent seventeen-year-old girl in the hands of a man like this. The trauma from this specific time of my abuse took a long time to heal from. I was programmed to take pain, listen to instructions, take orders, never speak and most importantly, never recall any of the events I witnessed or participated in. This resulted in full-blown dissociation.

Organised crime cults rely heavily on dissociation in their victims. They achieve it by inflicting extreme torture and pain, until the victim can't handle it anymore and mentally escapes, going somewhere else in their mind so they can't feel what is being done to their bodies.

Now let's pause for a moment and take a deep breath.
Most people are unfamiliar with mind control and extreme grooming, let alone organised crime cults, so this information can be challenging to accept. I mean, how could any of this happen at all, let alone to an innocent child? It's even worse to know that it can happen right under the noses of family and friends. But I can assure you that it does exist and there are many unsuspecting victims, just like me, who are ensnared and dragged down into them.

METAMORPHOSIS

On The Inside

I felt the drugs kicking in as he watched me.
Don't think. Follow orders. Say nothing. Comply or die.

I stood on the roadside as headlights appeared in the distance, penetrating my sensitive and dilated eyes. With a racing heart, I sat in the backseat. It felt like an hour passed before we arrived at a nondescript building where I was told to get out and walk around the back. He walked behind me, instructing me every step of the way. Navigating a labyrinth of Emergency Exit doors, stairways and ladders, we entered a brightly lit, fully enclosed room.

I had arrived in hell itself.

I was now exposed to some of the darkest and most sinister individuals. I was in the guts of a sophisticated organised crime unit.

'Never speak. Never tell a soul. Do everything we tell you. You belong to us.'

The past years of abuse were nothing compared to what these people did to me. All of it was designed to reinforce their number one rule: never speak. Organised crime cults have no boundaries or limitations on their desires—no matter how grotesque, perverted or violent. You may have seen cults like this depicted in movies. They pale compared to the horrifying reality. In my years with this cult, any number of atrocities I witnessed would imprison a person for life. Instantly. The number one currency of these cults is power, and they achieve it through money from sex trafficking, blackmail and coercion.

I didn't stand a chance.

I was abused ritualistically, brought to private parties as a commodity, forced to collect information and documents from important individuals and used for a variety of depraved activities. On multiple occasions, I heard them discuss how they would conceal my death if it occurred. Feigned car accidents and missing person reports were just a couple. They stopped at nothing to extort me. I experienced zero empathy, sympathy or compassion from anyone.

I hid it all, acted normal because my life depended on it.

I had no other choice, or so I thought. I was living a dual reality. I was under a giant hypnotic spell.

I spoke earlier about dissociation. Well, this level of abuse tipped it right over into the abyss. I'd essentially tap out of the pain to the point of feeling nothing. I learned to become so numb, it was as if I had no physical body. While I was in this state, they programmed me to 'never speak or else'. I was made to feel completely worthless. I was fully controlled, a malleable slave.

METAMORPHOSIS

The Escape

One day, something remarkable happened.
A level of consciousness washed over me that I hadn't experienced before.

I went from being numb to the entire situation to attaining complete awareness of my environment. I could see what my abusers were doing, the manipulations and tricks they were using to keep me suppressed. The veil lifted enough for me to catch a glimpse. It was only for a short time, but it was enough for me to notice.

And what I saw horrified me.

Until that moment, I was so brainwashed I didn't recognise there was anything to escape from. I was instructed to come back to the cult willingly and under no duress. This is how mind control works.

When these people set out to groom and program someone, they're playing a long game. They need their victims to be so indoctrinated that they don't actually *think* about leaving. Cults never chase their victims or drag them back into the cult. That's completely against their rules. Instead, they use tried-and-true methods of mind control where their victims don't see escape as an option.

The moment I woke up, I felt an overwhelming urge to

escape. I felt repulsed by everything I was surrounded by, and I knew I needed to run. I was twenty-one years old, and I was absolutely terrified.

To this day, I have no clue how or why my programming glitched the way it did. It was just for a brief window of time, but it was enough to break the spell and allow me to wake up. Years later, I bumped into people who knew him, and they told me that after I disappeared from his life, he was seen out on the street screaming obscenities about failed programming and looking like a haunted mess. These people had no idea what it meant, but I sure did.

One glimpse,
One slip of the veil,
And it was enough to wake me up
And break the spell.

PART TWO

My Healing

METAMORPHOSIS

The reality of my situation was this:
I never knew I needed to heal *until I started to heal*.

I'd developed complex coping mechanisms to function in the world. Most people would never suspect I had such a disturbing past. I was a high-functioning abuse victim who was good at hiding my truth and maintaining my facade.

After a decade of coping with life, something started to happen.
I started to *think* about my trauma.

Up until that time, I believed I'd reconciled my past, and life was as good as it was ever going to get. I had no idea anything better was even a possibility for me. The concept of healing was foreign, and I was just existing as best I could. But, at the age of thirty, the door to my past flung wide open, exposing all the painful memories that had been hidden away. I started to remember, feel, question and agonise over everything that had happened to me. Deep grief, anger, resentment and rage bubbled up as the atomic bomb of pain I was carrying prepared to explode.

I started to feel everything.

I became consumed with thoughts about my abusers, what they did to me, what they said to me, how they convinced me to believe them and how they manipulated and distorted my entire world. My mind was filled with images, flashbacks and horrifying moments I had buried, hoping to never confront them again.

> I couldn't stop it. I couldn't make it go away.
> It. Just. Happened.
> My mind, body and spirit had clearly decided it was time to revisit my past.

In the space of a month, I went from total avoidance of my trauma to an intense healing crisis that lasted approximately two years. During this time, I connected with and learned from some of the world's best psychologists, healers, doctors and shamans. I was on a mission to purge every atrocity I'd ever witnessed or participated in from my body. I stopped at nothing to release this newly emerged pain.

> Looking back, I can see that my trauma was ready to be released, and I was being given a clear choice:

> Let the memory of my rising trauma destroy me or start my healing journey now.
> I chose to heal.

Wave 1

Facing The Reality Of Your Past

I firmly believe in two things, and they've been proven to me over and over again.

1. Our bodies hold innate wisdom
2. We're never given anything we can't handle

The critical first step in releasing past pain from our bodies is confronting the objections of our minds. Specifically, those that tell us we're unworthy of being healed. These thoughts are barriers that hinder our progress and keep us locked into false narratives.

Put simply, these beliefs are just not true.

So many of us have had to live in a twisted version of reality, conforming to someone else's narrative in order to survive. In Wave 1, we work on recognising and releasing these as we set ourselves up for the journey ahead. We address the reality and aftermath of dealing with an abuser and I share concepts, techniques and thought-provoking questions to help you navigate out of their 'reality' and into your own.

In this wave, we discuss:
- Challenging the false beliefs implanted by others
- Questioning reality and discerning fact from fiction
- Recognising you were a victim, and releasing attachment to the victim persona
- Releasing internalised guilt and shame
- Gaining a different perspective and reframing your trauma

Let's begin.

Reasons To Heal

The more we ignore our trauma,
the more trauma we create.

Unprocessed trauma can be a powerful negative force in our lives, even when we're not consciously aware of it. While our trauma remains unhealed, we continue to attract that which we're trying so hard to escape from. Our trauma is like a magnet for toxic experiences, situations and people—essentially, everything we don't want to experience.

Sounds harsh, doesn't it? But allow me to explain.

Our natural inclination is to gravitate to the familiar. We seek comfort in patterns and behaviours we recognise because we consider them safer than the unknown. It's a survival instinct that has served us well throughout history, but it becomes problematic when we're dealing with trauma. Because, with trauma, if something 'feels' comfortable and familiar to us, it's a pretty safe bet it isn't healthy. The truth is, so many of us respond to our lives from a place of deep trauma. We're constantly re-enacting past hurts and repeating old storylines on a loop. But doing this is like letting the traumatised version of ourselves take the wheel while we become a passive passenger. We're disconnecting from our own power and aligning ourselves to our pain.

This is exactly what happened to me.

For years after I escaped, I found myself entangled with people who weren't good. Time and again, I attracted these toxic, unsavoury characters into my life. Don't get me wrong, I had no clue I was doing it, and even less of a clue they were unhealthy! These situations simply affirmed my world view and aligned with my past experiences. It was how life was.

See what I mean about familiarity?

Our deep attachment to our trauma stories and our alignment with victimhood plays such an integral role in our healing. We have to be ready to completely release the old, familiar patterns that are comfortable to us so we can move forward. Because while our trauma lives inside our minds and bodies, it's constantly reverberating outward through our behaviours, actions and energy. This means healing our trauma doesn't just benefit us, it flows through to our loved ones, family and friends, too. If we carry a lot of unprocessed traumas, we emit it constantly, and it affects the behaviour of others around us and toward us. If left unresolved, it can keep rippling out indefinitely. The good news is we can stop it. We just need to take full

responsibility.
This is my challenge to you.

View every day from this point forward as an opportunity to be courageous, conscious and open to transforming as an act of kindness towards yourself and those around you. You have the ability to jump back into the driver's seat of your life and once you do, you'll meet the real you. And so will your loved ones.

While you're going through this journey, I want you to think not only of yourself, but of the people you care about, too. What does your healing mean to them?

Imagine what a gift it would be for them to see you thriving, full of joy and living your best life?

The Reality Check We All Need

It's time to stop running and start healing.

*After all, this is your life we're talking about.
Is there anything more worthy of your commitment
and your time?*

Think about this for a moment. If someone breaks their leg, they typically seek medical attention, receive a prognosis and initiate a treatment plan to repair their broken bones. Depending on the severity of the injury, they might have to wear a cast, undergo surgery or spend weeks in rehab learning how to safely regain the use of their leg. If we met this person, would we classify or define them solely based on their injury? And should they carry the burden of guilt and shame forever because they once broke a limb? I don't say this to compare a broken leg with sexual abuse or paedophilia, and I'm certainly not trying to detract from the seriousness of the issue. But I can share that I have learned to see my trauma objectively. I now think of it as an injury, rather than a lifelong story of suffering and pain. Like the broken leg, it requires a serious and methodical treatment plan. And that plan starts with facing the truth.

Throughout this book, I refer to the concept of *'rethinking your trauma'*. This is a crucial part of releasing and healing because when we can see something from a different perspective, our bodies respond to it in a different way. We can use this in so many areas of our life, but it plays a huge role in releasing trapped trauma. For many of us, our attachment to our pain is a vice-like death grip. Rethinking it is the art of learning how to release, bit by bit, with intention and respect.

Rethinking doesn't mean dismissing.

The first step to rethinking your trauma is to take a good, hard look at the hand you've been dealt. And when I say a good look, I mean unflinching. I'm asking you to look beyond the facades your mind has constructed and to navigate your deeply embedded stories and false beliefs. Why do I say false? Because you were made to accept them as truth. It can be difficult to know the difference at this stage, but here's a clue. Anything telling you that you're unlovable, unworthy or so broken you'll never be healed? That's not the truth. That's a story your abuser wants you to believe.

Throughout this book, I guide you to delve deeper into these stories and facades. Some were implanted by others, some we created ourselves to cope with what was happening, but they all need to be released. For now, just knowing they exist and sitting with that knowledge is enough.

My reality check

When I took an unflinching look at my past, I was horrified by my ultimate truth. I was sold a giant lie. Now this wasn't any *small* lie. It was a lie that shaped my entire belief system and way of life for over two decades. When I had the courage to examine it for what it truly was, my truth was confronting and brutal.

I was the victim of a paedophile.
Nothing more, and nothing less.
Huge reality check. Shattering, if I'm honest.

I grappled with this truth for a very long time, and I found myself plagued by questions that had no answers. Every word spoken, every action taken, every single moment of my life had been a predatory act to manipulate me.

As unbelievable as it was, I had to reconcile the fact that I'd been played. Yes, I had been groomed and programmed since I was a child. But that didn't make it any easier. This was not the truth I wanted. Part of me still wanted to believe the lie. But when it comes to the truth, there is simply no arguing with it.

Taking the first step

It takes time to relinquish all the deeply held, false beliefs that tell us we're willing participants in our own mistreatment or abuse. It requires a willingness to confront things we may have been groomed to completely reject. Here are some thought-starters to ease you into the idea of challenging these long-held beliefs. I suggest you approach everything from the angle of 'what if?'. There's no shame in being uncomfortable with this process or feeling a strong resistance to it the first time around. At this point, we're just gently exploring what's possible, so take all the time you need.

Ask yourself:
- They told me they loved me. Is it possible that they could have been lying?
- Is it possible the person I thought cared about me could have been manipulating my feelings for their gain?
- Is it possible this person isn't who I thought they were?
- Could I have been coerced or manipulated into believing something that isn't true?

Your truth may be the same as mine, or it may be completely different. But here's the thing. This healing journey is the most important thing you're going to do in your life, so this is not the time to shy away. This is the time to be brave and confront your truth, whatever that may be. You've already decided you want to heal your trauma and build a new life. Would you rather build it on an unstable foundation of lies? Or a solid foundation of truth?

Accepting the reality of our situation is the first step to unlocking the truth about ourselves. When we no longer carry around someone else's stories and false beliefs about love, care and devotion, we open the space to form our own. This is the first and most important step towards our own healing.

METAMORPHOSIS

Grooming Versus Reality

Trauma is the systematic numbing of our feelings to prevent us from connecting with who we truly are.

One day, approximately ten years after my abuse had ended, I felt a growing need to confide. This was a strange feeling because I'd spent years guarding my secrets and keeping myself locked up like a vault. But now I had the urge to share my story with someone I could trust.

Tentatively, I began to reveal tiny snippets of information to those I was closest to, the smallest disclosures about my past. Each time I opened up and revealed something, the reaction was always the same.

'You know that's not normal, right?'
'You should report him immediately.'
'This person is a psychopath.'

My response was always the same, too ...
'That's just how he was.'
'He was an eccentric character.'

Like so many abuse victims, I couldn't see the predatory intent behind his actions. I'd been groomed so effectively it was like I had blinkers on. Fast forward ten years and that same programming was *still* preventing me from thinking clearly about what I'd experienced. I mean, I knew it was wrong, and of course I was incredibly relieved to have escaped, but I still struggled to accept the truth of my situation. It continued to cloud my judgement and prevent me from accepting the facts. My grooming said, *'Nothing to see here.'* Reality said, *'Everything was a lie. He abused you.'*

An outside perspective told me how twisted and wrong the whole thing was, but I'd never thought of it like this. And, for the first time, it was quite hard to accept. My 'special' and 'unique' relationship was textbook paedophilia.

I created a list of questions to remove my blinkers and help me see how targeted I was. You may find these questions helpful when trying to discern reality from fiction:

- Did this person make me feel special and unique?
- Did they make me feel isolated, different or superior from family and friends?
- Were they overly invested in me?
- Were they always trying to get me alone?
- Did they have an instant or unusually strong rapport with me?
- Did I trust this person?
- Did I follow their lead without question?
- Did I laugh at their jokes and comments, even if it felt wrong?
- Did this person touch me in any way? And did it feel strange?
- Did I want to say no, but felt like I couldn't?
- Did I agree to do things around this person which were out of character?
- Did I feel embarrassed, or bottle things up?
- Did I ever feel oppressed, or afraid to be who I really was?
- Was I afraid of disappointing this person?

When I did this exercise, I answered yes to all the questions. My situation was, without a doubt, a calculated attack.

This realisation was more of a reality than anything I was told by him.

I encourage you to complete the same exercise or create your own set of questions to broaden your perspective. What we're trying to do is apply a filter of logic and sense to a situation where there is none. Doing an exercise like this can help you gain a better understanding and become more clinical and pragmatic when thinking about your trauma, which will serve you well as we navigate this healing journey.

Is It Fiction Or Fact?

My faith and belief in myself are stronger than my attachment to the pain that was inflicted upon me.

Confronting an abusive past can feel like gruelling work, and many false narratives pop up and make themselves known. But the more we pull on that thread of truth, the more those narratives fall apart until, eventually, every lie woven into the fabric of our abuse is exposed.

I held so many beliefs planted by my abuser that seeped into my vulnerable teenage brain and lodged themselves there, just as he intended. He chose his words carefully and repeated them to me over and over again:

- What we have is special and meaningful
- You'll never find another connection like this one
- You're a very complex and special person who only I can understand
- No one loves you like I do
- No one will care for you like I do
- No one will ever be able to truly understand you like I do
- I love you

Through the deliberate use of language, they construct an artificial and distorted reality in order to manipulate. This is the glue that binds us to them and allows them full control. Often, they'll affirm that the physical and psychological abuse is 'true, devotional love'. This is a complete distortion of the truth and only serves to reinforce the abuser's behaviour. This is how toxic and twisted it is. It isn't love at all. It is manipulation.

For every abuse victim, a foundation was laid first, serving as a stable base for further abuse to build upon. This foundation can take many forms, including physical punishment, neglect or emotional deprivation. For me, it was false 'love' and exclusivity.

In order to rethink my trauma, I had to apply a cognitive frame that what I was being told was not truthful. If I held onto false narratives, I was never going to completely heal, so being able to recognise false statements and how they affected me was critical. While I had no reliable barometer for the truth, I did have logic. And I learned to apply it to distinguish fact from fiction.

I asked myself these conceptual questions:
- If love is always associated with physical pain, is it really love? Or could it possibly be something else?
- Could the people who abused me really be the only

people in a world of billions who could actually love me? Is that statistically truthful?
- What if what they told me isn't the truth at all?
- What if they needed me to believe they loved me in order to protect themselves?
- I knew that if I wanted a normal, grounded relationship one day, I couldn't regress to that way of thinking again. I'd need a plan to navigate my own red flags.

I asked myself:
- Do I attempt to bring certain behaviours into new relationships? (E.g., Nodding, smiling, giggling and the controlling dynamics)
- Do I look for similar attention to that which I received in the past?
- Do I feel superior to my partner because I was continually told I was better than others?
- Do I feel any kind of shame about having a normal relationship?

Using these questions and applying logic to them, I began to release the firmly held beliefs planted within me. I then affirmed to myself that the type of care I needed was not one that kept me believing I was broken and wounded. I'd simply been convinced that I did.

Once my eyes opened to this lie, I began to rewrite what was truthful to myself.

So, I ask you:
- What are the foundational lies you were told?
- What were the false beliefs that surrounded this lie?
- How can you rewrite these beliefs to align with what is truthful to you?

PART TWO WAVE ONE

To Forgive Or Not To Forgive

You were made to accept it, but you no longer have to carry it.

When we awaken to the truth of our past, many of the beliefs we hold about ourselves and the world around us crumble. We may feel shock, betrayal, disbelief and distrust, or that we don't know what's real and what isn't anymore.

For me, the very foundation of my life now felt rocky and unstable. To move forward, I had to construct an entirely new foundation that was solid, uncompromising and based on love. But how could I when my experiences of romantic love were so toxic?

I could do it through radical, deep, compassionate forgiveness.

You see, if we hold a belief that we are even *partially* to blame for what happened to us, it is detrimental to healing. We must completely and wholeheartedly distance ourselves from *any* blame when it comes to our abuse.

At this point, you may need to stop and feel into your body.
- Do you feel in any way, no matter how small, that you are to blame?
- Does any part of you feel that, on some level, you must have 'agreed' to participate?

The difference in the two statements is subtle, but both lines of thought are equally dangerous. This was a dilemma I battled over and over again. I mean, I kept complying with his requests and I never reported him or told anyone about it, so how was I not complicit in the whole thing? I must be responsible for some of the abuse that took place, right? Wrong.

I never, ever, ever asked to be abused. And neither did you.

I was a child with no ability to recognise manipulation, coercion and brainwashing. Why would I? How could I consent to these things when I wasn't even aware of them as concepts? Waking up to the truth of your past is one thing, but forgiving your part in it is quite another. However, it's absolutely crucial and I can't stress this enough.

We don't need to carry the blame for their actions.

Think about this for a moment. Grooming and brainwashing work so effectively on children because we're all born with inherent purity, innocence and goodness. This is fundamentally who we are. Those who seek to harm, mistreat or groom us use various methods to separate us from this truth, including:
- Making us take on the shame and guilt of what happened
- Making us accept the blame for the abuse
- Having us agree to be silent for fear of being caught or to protect their reputation
- Having us agree to be silent for fear of our loved ones being hurt
- Making us preserve the relationship between us and them

All of this goes against our innate human nature. If we were any of the things they wanted us to believe (horrible, shameful, etc.), all the effort they put into programming us wouldn't be necessary, would it?

Why is this important? Because we can't rethink our trauma and experience complete healing if we're carrying self-judgement, guilt or shame. We must remember that we're all born with goodness in our hearts. We are not the things they told us, and we certainly don't need to carry their shame and guilt. In my experience, once I reaffirmed that I never wanted the abuse and I never would have agreed to any of it, I began to separate myself from the false belief that I was an active and guilty participant in my abuse, to the real truth, that I was a child who was preyed upon by a sexual predator. And it wasn't my fault.

> To help cement this in my mind, I wrote out truth statements like the ones below.
> - An adult preyed upon my innocence as a child and teenager
> - My grooming made me think what he was doing was okay
> - My grooming prevented me from reporting the abuse
> - If my parents knew about it, it never would have happened
> - If he wasn't in my life, I never would have been introduced to the things I was made to do. I never would have sought them out

I encourage you to write out your own truth statements to affirm you are not to blame for your abuse. This belief needs to be crystal clear and unwavering if you want to truly let go of shame and guilt.

And on the topic of forgiveness, have you ever heard the advice, 'Just forgive them and move on'? Me too. And if you're anything like me, you want to tear your hair out. How can you be expected to forgive and move on after everything they did? Wouldn't that be letting them off the hook? It feels so fundamentally wrong, so how do you do it? I struggled with this for a long time before I found an approach that worked.

What I came to realise is this:
It's not about forgiveness, it's about perspective.

Those who choose to perpetrate abuse on others often have a history of being abused themselves. While they may not outwardly exhibit signs of their own pain and suffering, they act out of a deep-seated need to cope with their own unresolved trauma. For some, the only way to do this is to inflict pain on others and perpetuate a cycle they weren't strong enough to break. Unfortunately for us, we end up in their firing line. I never forgave. But in time, I came to see them in a different light which helped me forgive their actions. They were simply re-enacting what they knew. Once I grasped this concept, I began to imagine the unprocessed trauma, the anger and the self-loathing to be able to hurt people in the way they did. It was possible they had been tortured and tormented and didn't have the tools, support or courage to heal. Instead, they chose to perpetuate the abuse. Deciding to approach forgiveness in this way isn't always easy, but it helped me move beyond the narrative of 'I need to forgive' to a place where I could forgive the action and recognise it as part of a painful cycle.

Pause now and think about it for a moment.

Our approach to forgiveness and the process of deciding how we forgive those who hurt us is of utmost importance. Forgiveness is not a simple or straightforward act. It requires us to delve deep into our past experiences, identify and confront the pain and trauma inflicted upon us and recognise the underlying reasons that may have led to it (in this case, someone else choosing to perpetuate abuse). Forgiveness demands us to be intentional in our approach and can lead to a greater sense of compassion, both for ourselves and for those who have hurt us.

It may take time, but one day you will be so healed that you feel deep compassion for your abusers and, most importantly, yourself.

A Huge Change In Perception

My abusers were the ones who were scared.

As we move away from a place of blame and towards a place of compassion, a deep and significant truth begins to surface. How much anxiety did they feel while managing us, their victims? Allow me to explain.

In my situation, I was sold a giant lie around love, when the truth had nothing to do with love, and everything to do with keeping me small and subservient. Why? So that I always remained compliant and abused. *By them.* Remember, abusers capitalise on our vulnerabilities and use anything they can to keep us small and controlled because they can't risk us leaving or reporting them. The idea of us regaining our power and self-worth? Well, that's an abuser's worst nightmare.

So, with that in mind, take a moment to consider how your abuser needed you. Until now, you've probably never thought of it this way, right? In fact, you likely felt dependent on them. But what if this was always an inversion of the truth? What if they depended on us? What if they never really knew if they were safe to abuse us or not? What if they were just as scared of what we could do to them as we were of what they were doing to us?

This. Is. Huge.

Reframing the abuse in this way can help us realise we had much more power than we were ever led to believe. This paradigm shift is the basis for recognising and claiming our self-worth. We all have a fundamental desire to know that we matter, that our words and actions mean something, and we have some value in this world, but abuse strips all of this away. Perhaps for the first time ever, you may recognise that you do, in fact, have more power than you know.

So, I'm asking you now:
- How did they minimise you?
- How anxious did they feel about being caught?
- How scared do you think they were of you rather than you of them?
- How much of their control was actually an illusion?

PART TWO WAVE ONE

I Gave My Word, But I Didn't Mean It

A guilty person never speaks up.

We've made some great progress so far, but now I'd like to talk about embracing our freedom and letting go of implanted negative beliefs so we can dive into the cool, clear waters of healing.

I understand how difficult this can be, especially when faced with memories of things we've been led to believe we did consensually. We might even think, *'How did I ever agree to that? Why would I have said yes? Why was I so willing?'* The truth is, you weren't willing at all. You were likely groomed, manipulated, coerced or physically forced.

You see, when an abuser grooms someone for abuse, they build up trust and create false emotional connections they use to manipulate us with at a later stage. They may indoctrinate us so much we go against our intuition and free will. It starts with small things, but once trust has been gained, an abuser keeps ratcheting up the dial. Before we know it, we're completely under their spell, impressionable, malleable and ripe for exploitation. They make us absorb the guilt and carry the shame to ensure our silence. A guilty and shameful person never speaks up.

In my situation, I was made to accept one hundred per cent of the guilt, every single drop of it, all the time. Being guilty and shameful were such natural emotions for me, I almost didn't feel like myself without them. I didn't understand what it meant for others to take responsibility as a result—a key lesson we discuss in the final wave of this book. I carried the burden of these emotions with me for years post-abuse. It's been a continuous process to shift them, even after I started my healing journey. The river of abuse runs very deep.

We often don't know that we've taken on someone else's guilt and shame because it's such a habitual pattern for us. But there are real implications for taking on excessive emotions that don't belong to us.

In my case, I'd been dragging these burdens around with me for years. Was I going to take this guilt and shame with me to the grave? No. I reflected deeply on how the guilt got there and I came to this conclusion. I was coerced to accept the guilt and shame. It was 'unwilling consent', and it had been weaponised against me. Pennies started to drop! In order to survive everything I went through, I *had* to accept blame, shame and guilt. It was a lie, but one I had to play along with to keep myself alive. The problem was, even though I'd escaped my abusers years earlier, I still carried what I'd been coerced to accept. I allowed their shameful deeds to stay with me and weigh me down.

It was time to lighten my load.
How did I release the guilt and shame?

I concluded that if I gave my unwilling consent then, I could reverse it through conscious *non*-consent now. I spoke the words loudly and clearly.

'I do not consent.'

I began to apply this when I thought about the experiences, all the actions, words and deeds I was coerced into that had filled me with shame. I replayed the abusive events in my mind and focused on sending out a very clear, strong intention while doing so. Again, I spoke the words aloud.

'I do not consent.'

I revisited all the oaths I was forced to take and the actions I carried out that were against my will. I rescinded them too.

'I do not consent.'

I'd been made to absorb all this guilt and shame, but now I wanted to release it all. I wanted to take my power back.

To release guilt and shame, we must first identify and clarify our relationship to it. Where does it show up in our day-to-day life? What type of guilt were we made to take on? Do we feel guilty for what happened to us? All we need at this point is awareness and a recognition that perhaps we're operating through a lens of guilt and shame. When we're aware, we can no longer be controlled by it, and that's wonderful progress for this stage of our healing.

METAMORPHOSIS

The Perfect Healing Timeline Doesn't Exist

I shall not seek to 'finish' my healing, but rather seek to live my life where inner peace and freedom are my metric.

Healing from trauma is one of the most complex, difficult, challenging, rewarding and personal things someone can do, but it's not a linear journey! Ups and downs are to be expected, and you may reach a milestone one day, then feel like you've taken ten steps back the next. While this is frustrating, the important thing to remember is this:

Each person's journey toward healing is entirely unique and cannot be compared to anyone else's.

What works for you may not work for someone else. There is no single 'right' way to heal. It takes time, patience and a willingness to confront difficult emotions and memories. Wading through the muddy waters of deceit and lies is gruelling, but I promise you that waiting for you on the other side is a sense of peace and healing that is uniquely your own.

In my journey, I experienced a healing crisis that lasted two years and, believe it or not, I had people ask me why it was taking so long! In the early days, I felt weak and inadequate hearing this. Later, I realised I had to let those feelings go and let my body's natural intelligence do what it needed in order to heal. The reality of healing deep trauma is we have a degree of cognitive control over our healing, but our body has much more of a say. When I let go of the idea of the perfect healing timeline, and allowed whatever to come up when it did, my healing sped up. Why? Because I stopped judging the process and trying to control how fast it should be happening. In this journey, attaching ourselves to a fixed timeline does more harm than good. How long it takes, what comes up, and when are parameters we can never control.

So, if there's no finish line, and we can't control the parameters, how do we know when we're getting closer to being healed?

We can measure our progress.

I became aware of this almost by accident when I noticed I could do certain things more easily than I had in the past. They were milestones I'd never qualified, but were incredibly important to me:

- I could share my story without intense, overwhelming emotion
- I could share my story without feeling like I was putting myself in danger
- I became familiar with what triggered me and what was 'safe' to be around
- I cried in solitude for what I went through, but I no longer felt drained by the painful memories (compared to earlier where I would cry myself into an exhausted sleep)
- I went from being depressed often to having short bouts that only lasted a few hours
- I started to believe I was worthy of a loving relationship
- I started to allow myself the opportunity to let good men lead me from my painful past, and I allowed

men around me to show me love
- My nightmares, night sweats, flashbacks and sleep apnoea significantly reduced
- I became more accepting of strong feelings like grief, anger or injustice. I learned to accept and sit with them

Even though it didn't feel like I was getting anywhere, I was making progress.

When it comes to healing, no magical finish line suddenly appears. It's a continuous journey that becomes more manageable with effort and time. That's why it's essential to pause and reflect on the progress you make. It's possible to overlook your achievements without realising.

Think about this for a moment:
- Are there activities that used to be extremely difficult but now come easily to you?
- Are there areas where you feel stronger than you felt a week ago, a month ago, or a year ago?

Perhaps for the first time, you may be considering that you're not what your abuser said you were at all. When you recognise this, you're on the path of a truly metamorphic healing journey.

Remember, it takes as long as it takes. The key is to not lose hope. Have nothing but complete faith in your ability to meet what lies ahead. This opens you up to complete and whole healing and, frankly, you deserve nothing less than that.

PART TWO WAVE ONE

Return To Self

You will be restored with so much more than you lost.

When I started to unravel my brainwashing, grooming and long-held beliefs, it felt like my life was unravelling too. Everything I'd once held onto was now coming undone. This was both daunting and disorienting because my world began to look completely different.

I had to surrender everything I *thought* was true to make room for what actually was.
This was not an easy transition.

Even though I had such deep-rooted misconceptions about love, connection, and relationships, this warped and distorted reality was the only one I knew. Surrendering it felt insurmountable at times. I had to keep connecting back to my belief in myself and my deep desire to fully heal. In other words, I had to let go of the old to make way for the new. I promise you, there is a point where we see this unravelling as a gift, something to lead us out of our suffering to a place where we have control of our lives. I looked at it as the first sign that I had agreed to completely surrender. My world was shifting from one of slavery and trauma to one of love and freedom. And that can only be a good thing. As we rethink our trauma, enhance our day-to-day life and find forgiveness, acceptance and self-love, there may be moments where it seems almost unbearable to continue. But trust that the events of our past cannot hurt us today. As we let go of our old trauma storylines and focus on constructing and magnetising an abundant new reality to us, we'll have one foot in each world until it feels safe enough to fully take the leap.

You are safe.

Before we dive into Wave 2, understand that we're not changing ourselves. We're releasing layers of false beliefs and programming around who we were forced to be, and coming back to who we really are.

Let's continue on this incredible journey together.

Wave 2
Navigating The Rollercoaster Of Healing

*I want you to feel so healed, it's almost as if your
abuse took place in another lifetime.
That is my wish for you. That is where I want you to be.*

In Wave 1, we focused on techniques to help reframe our past, discern fact from fiction and recognise the false beliefs implanted by our abusers, such as feeling unworthy of healing because we participated in our abuse. Doing this work is crucial because, once we dissolve these beliefs, we can open ourselves up to the second wave of healing.

Wave 2 is about being in the trenches. This is one of the most turbulent and challenging stages, but it provides the biggest opportunity for spiritual growth and expansion.

We look at:
- Recognising and releasing toxic cravings and desires
- Breaking the people-pleasing cycle
- What to expect physically when releasing severe or prolonged trauma

METAMORPHOSIS

---

*Note to reader: This Wave can be particularly triggering because it reveals whether our trauma is more entrenched than we first imagined. If you feel overwhelmed or overstimulated at any point, I encourage you to stop, put the book down, go for a walk and breathe fresh air. There's no rush when it comes to healing. We must be gentle with ourselves and aware of what we can and can't handle.

Uncovering our trapped traumas, unconscious patterns and behaviours is like opening Pandora's box, especially when we see just how many of them still linger in the present day. It's natural for the events of the past to influence the way we perceive the world, make decisions, and interact with others, but the impact is particularly profound for survivors of violent and ongoing abuse. Wave 2 addresses the string of psychological consequences and behavioural traits that can emerge from these adverse experiences.

There were moments during this part of my journey where I had to stop digging into my trauma and take a break from *the healing*. I needed time to absorb what I was learning about myself and integrate it with what I was trying to heal from. My attitude towards healing fluctuated wildly during this time. I'd go from feeling confident I could navigate the healing process one moment to intense disbelief that I had any sort of capacity to overcome it the next! My journey was never a straight line. Only I knew how much I could handle at any given time. I had to be the gatekeeper of my healing, so, while I never gave up, I had to take breaks. I encourage you to be gentle with yourself as we move through this stage.

PART TWO WAVE TWO

The Healing Trifecta

Self-healing is a skill best managed with strong, unwavering intent.

I discovered three key concepts that set the foundation for a safe, balanced and grounded healing journey and I'd like to share them with you:
- Belief
- Worthiness
- Trust

Your *belief* that you can heal must override all the other false beliefs you encounter along the way and anchor you when your trauma feels overwhelming and insurmountable. Your belief needs to be solid, unflinching and stronger than any pain or difficulty that may arise.

Your *self-worth* is something you need to reinforce constantly because entertaining thoughts of shame and guilt will derail your progress. Whenever you feel this narrative arising, take a moment to reframe your thoughts around the past. Revisit the concepts in Wave 1 and remind yourself of the truth—you are innocent in all of this. The good news is the more you heal, the more you feel worthy of being healed. You simply have to start somewhere.

Lastly, you're on this journey because you're ready to be here, so *trust* you're being shown only what you're ready to see. If you're experiencing a symptom, trust that your body, in all its infinite wisdom, has presented it for you to experience and release.

Our bodies and minds are capable of remarkable things and assist us, sometimes even taking over our healing in their own natural way, if we let them. Trauma needs to come out of the body, mind and spirit. If we stifle it, we only delay its release. It's going to come out eventually. Better to trust and honour the time our bodies have chosen and embrace it when it arrives.

The Truth About Fear

Everything that haunts me is based on fear.
Remove the fear, and the haunting stops.

Now we understand the importance of keeping our *belief*, *worthiness* and *trust* in balance, let's look at the antithesis to this—fear.

I'm a firm believer in fear having its place. It's a natural evolutionary response and exists for a reason. Fear is a prevalent emotion when it comes to trauma healing and, if mismanaged, can bring our progress to a screeching halt. But when handled correctly and with care, it can fuel some of our greatest breakthroughs. We should never completely disregard our fear because, when in balance, it's our ally. Fear always has something important to tell us. The problem is people who abuse us have appropriated our fear and used it to manipulate and control us. So, what was once a personal safety mechanism and natural response is now wildly out of balance. For many of us, our fear has been running the show.

PART TWO WAVE TWO

Fear, in proportion, is our ally.
Fear that has been programmed into us is an illusion.

Abusers like to take fear, twist it to their advantage and wield it like a freshly sharpened weapon. This is what I refer to as 'Extra Programmed Fear'. This type of fear is so insidious, it needs to be separated from natural fear and pulled out like a weed. Programming these extra fears often starts with threats to our safety or those of our loved ones. You've no doubt heard them before:

'If you tell anyone about this, you'll be punished.'
'If you tell your family, they will all be killed.'
'Everyone will know what you've done if you say a word.'

I had a lot of programmed fears I needed to extract, so I asked myself these questions:
- Do I still believe I'll be hurt if I speak out?
- When I speak about my trauma, do I feel immense fear?
- Does it ring true for me that my family and friends would have blamed me for what happened to me? Would they have turned against me, or would they have reported that person and protected me?
- Do I have excessive fears that are difficult to manage at times?
- If someone encourages me to report my abuser, do I feel defensive or fearful? If so, why?

I began to see the extent to which my fear had been manipulated and how it had kept me debilitated for so long. I worked on dismantling the beliefs that had developed as a result of these added fears, which led to a newfound sense of freedom and equilibrium within my body. When we systematically shed the excessive fears we carry, we begin to experience life with our fear levels in balance, and our innate, natural fears (the ones that keep us safe and protected in dangerous situations) become the only ones that guide us.

Holding fear within the body requires a large amount of energy and keeps us in a constant state of fight or flight, overworking the adrenals and depleting us. This is why, when we do healing work, we often feel lighter, more energised and more invigorated. We're energetically 'lightening our load' and releasing the burden of these ingrained and programmed 'extra' fears. Remember, our bodies are always trying to restore equilibrium. When given the opportunity, the body, mind and spirit work together to release the fear and restore balance.

So That's Where That Comes From

Unpacking our trauma means unpacking the subconscious desires and cravings connected to our abuse.

It's important we become aware of just how much our fear could be driving our choices. If left unchecked, programmed fear can lead to behaviour that seems incongruous with our true selves, causing us to act in ways that don't align with our values or beliefs. Let's break this down.

If we think about a past abusive situation, pleasing that

person meant doing what they wanted us to do, whether we wanted to or not. In other words, we were 'pleasing' for fear of being punished. On a deep subconscious level, we created values and beliefs that fuelled our choices, which were inherently backed by fear and trauma. In my case, someone else's ideology and sensationalist ideas heavily influenced me, so it shouldn't be any surprise that they influenced my subconscious desires, too. I learned from a young age that 'going along' with his requests and desires was far easier than rejecting them. I lived in fear of him all the time, and I didn't even know it.

Reflecting deeper, I not only learned to agree with his views, I adopted them and made them my own. Due to the addictive nature of grooming, I learned what would appease him and gain me the extra attention I was groomed to seek, whether it was dressing a certain way or agreeing to partake in abusive activities. I was programmed to crave reward, approval, compliments or elevated status. It was a toxic dynamic that had a deep and lasting effect.

An abusive dynamic like this sets up unhealthy expectations. Many of us have felt forced to adopt ideologies and participate in activities that were not for our highest good.

This led to other things, such as:
- Hyper-sexualisation
- Self-objectification
- Addictions that are dangerous to our health

These behaviours and fear-based desires lead to dysfunction and chaos in our lives if left uncurbed. Why is this so important? Because oftentimes we're still operating from these fear-based, wounded parts of ourselves while our true selves are buried underneath, waiting for us to dissolve the false desires and set them free.

While on my healing journey, I started to unpack the other subconscious ideas and programs running silently in the back of my mind. I wanted to ensure my life was mine, and no longer influenced by what those who abused me wanted me to be, say or do. I needed to cultivate enough self-awareness to discern when I was making a choice for myself, and when I was re-enacting trauma and wounding. To identify the difference, I asked myself these questions, which helped me choose what I genuinely desired in my heart versus the fear-based desires planted in my mind.

- Do I feel an overwhelming compulsion to do something, even if my gut says it isn't quite right?
- Do I make choices according to fantasies playing out in my mind? E.g., If I listen to this music, I'm reminded of past times when I was validated?
- Am I re-enacting anything today that they suggested I do?
- Do I find myself drawn to certain activities they told me I was good at?
- Do I crave a certain type of attention when I'm in an altered state? E.g., Does drinking cause me to crave being spoken to like they spoke to me?

Another way to identify if we're running wounded programs and patterns is to question any decision that we feel *extra* energised about. Becoming acutely aware of the process behind any decision-making allows us to draw in much healthier experiences, affirming that we are back in control of our choices.

PART TWO WAVE TWO

The Body Remembers, Even If The Mind Forgets

Our bodies contain trillions of cells, each one containing a memory, a charge. Where there is excess charge, we become dense and heavy. We must clear and restore this back to balance, and that is done through deep self-work.

It's clear that fear is at the root of many of our self-destructive behaviours and choices. When we ask ourselves the confronting question, 'Why would we ever want to recreate a situation or scenario from our abusive past?', we have no choice but to ask the follow-up question, 'Could there be something deeper at play here?' The answer, of course, is *yes*, and it lies in the chemical cellular connection we have to that experience. You see, it's not just our minds that hold the memory of trauma and fear, it's also our bodies. I call it *imprinting* and it's an important topic to understand because it can help set us free.

Our first sexual experiences *imprint* our sexuality and set the tone for what our body deems pleasurable in the future, something paedophiles take advantage of with early grooming. When a paedophile touches a minor, their body can automatically respond positively, even if the mind is in shock and fear. In fact, it's not unheard of for victims to experience orgasm during times of abuse. The encounter gets imprinted, and the victim now associates intimacy and pleasure with a person dominating them or touching them sexually without permission or consent. The abuser can keep introducing sexual acts and more extreme abuse scenarios, and you have one seriously strong sexual imprint. The minor could grow up to be an adult with a craving to be punished or treated violently, even if it is done with consent. The unconscious desire and behaviour are fed purely from the chemical cellular connection to their earlier sexual experiences. By re-enacting their sexual imprinting, they strengthen the imprint, deepen the underlying (unconscious) fears and re-traumatise themselves over and over again. It's a vicious loop where the victim becomes self-perpetrating. Our sexual desires are just one example, but this type of abusive imprinting can extend across many other areas of our lives.

Our Bodies Give Us Clues, We Just Have To Listen

Any imprint, whether traumatic or positive, leaves an impression on the brain. The brain is somewhat of a soft sponge. Therefore, by this assumption, we must drop any belief that trauma is permanent and replace it with the thought that positive work and self-development equally, and just as drastically, affect the brain.
In short, we can assume that just as we are easily traumatised, we are as easily cured.

The human body's capacity to retain and recall experiences can be both a blessing and a curse. The good news is, it can direct our attention to all aspects of ourselves that are unhealed, provided we're willing to listen. Essentially, our bodies can serve as an early warning system to prevent us from causing further harm to ourselves. The more attuned we are to our feelings, the more accurately we can receive the messages our bodies are trying to send us. We need to be mindful of the strong sensations that arise and examine them with honesty and self-awareness.

Here are some questions to help you discern whether the desire you feel in the moment is yours or an imprint:
- Do I feel embodied in this moment? Or could I be dissociated?
- Do I feel extra energised, or even manic, about doing a certain activity or buying a certain item? If so, why?
- What activities do I participate in (whether sexually or recreationally) that leave me feeling empty or dissociated? Do these activities feel truly loving? Or could they be imprinted desires?
- What strange cravings do I have that could be connected to my abuse?
- What desires do I have that seem out of character for me? For example, do I desire to be a bikini model or show off my body when I'm actually quite a conservative person?

I remember meeting a man once who identified as completely heterosexual but felt sexually attracted to men. He had no desire to follow through on his attraction or become romantic with a man, but he constantly battled an insatiable sexual desire that he wished never existed. As I got to know him more, I discovered he was molested by a man when he was a young boy. His first sexual imprint was with a man, so while his mind rejected the thought, his body retained the sensation. For this man, he had to heal the imprint that his body had retained and reprogram himself back to his authentic desires.

It takes time to unpack the imprinted desires buried in our subconscious, but simply being aware that they exist is the first step. And sometimes awareness is all we need for them to quite literally vanish. So, in all aspects of your life, it's helpful to acknowledge and tune into your feelings and constantly ask: Does this desire feel true to me?

You Can't Please Everyone

When you've been conditioned to give, it can be hard to receive, even when the 'receiving' is done graciously.

By now, it's probably clear that reclaiming power over minds and bodies is one of the most essential steps in our healing journey. We can't fully heal ourselves if we're still operating from our fears and wounds. Awareness and compassion are our much-needed allies as we learn how the past has shaped our minds and hijacked our feelings and emotions.

So where to now?

PART TWO WAVE TWO

Well. Very naturally. People-pleasing.

Now that we've looked into what drives our life decisions, let's discuss the underlying conditions, such as grooming, that drive our interactions with people. By now, you know I relied heavily on gaining approval, which meant I was hyper-vigilant to the merest hint of disapproval! If I made a mistake or caused disappointment, I was severely punished. My fear was constantly in the driver's seat.

No prizes for guessing how this translated to adulthood! My people-pleasing was well and truly off the charts. In fact, I was so highly attuned and sensitive to people's disappointment in me, it sent my body into an immediate stress response. My need for validation and my fear of rejection were equally strong. And while nothing's inherently wrong with wanting to make others happy, people pleasing becomes a problem when it's triggered by trauma and backed by fear. For most survivors of abuse, people-pleasing is yet another strategy we learned to keep ourselves safe. But it can prevent us from making authentic connections and lead to resentment.

> These questions helped me recognise where I was people-pleasing in my life:
> - Are there any situations in my life where I'm scared of making a mistake?
> - Do I prioritise making other people feel comfortable?
> - Do I always try to give the perfect answer or self-edit when speaking with others?
> - Do I put others' needs before my own?
> - Do I feel embarrassed about natural human things such as making a mess, being hungover, having a lover, or not being on time?

- Do I always do what others think is right, even if I don't think it is?
- Do I suppress how I feel for the sake of others?
- How do I feel when I don't abide by someone's requests?

If you recognise yourself in these questions, that's great, because it means you have a reference point to come back to. While there's no immediate 'off' switch for people-pleasing, you can learn to temper your tendencies and modify your behaviour patterns with awareness and self-compassion, so that the urge gradually fades. It took me a long time to deprogram this and be okay with not pleasing every single person around me. Regular journal entries helped break these patterns and elevate my awareness of the behaviour. Here, I would reflect on the following questions:

Did I over-commit this week?
How could I avoid doing this next time?

Did I agree to do something without thinking?
Could I have delayed this somehow?

Did I answer a question too fast without thinking?
Could I have taken a breath before answering?

Did I feel resentment or anger?
Could I have expressed it instead of repressing it?

Did I feel shameful over something small and struggle to let it go?
Could I have avoided this shame in the first place? Could I have invited more self-compassion at that moment?

Did I reach out for help when needed, or did I suppress the feelings inside?

I could clearly see how much, and in how many ways, I was people-pleasing (spoiler alert, it was much more than I realised). Through journalling and reflection, I learned to eventually recognise, in real time, when I was in danger of repeating ingrained behaviours. Although it was hugely uncomfortable and distressing to start with, the experience became quite enlightening the more I did it. I was no longer burdened by the pressure of being perfect or of doing things simply to please others. I could be my true, authentic self and if that meant disappointing someone else, then so be it.

Today, I fully embrace that not everyone likes me or approves of my behaviour, and that's okay. I now have the freedom to seek out and enjoy more authentic relationships.

To back my own words, to be self-approving is one of the greatest gifts after so much trauma and abuse.

Years of mindlessly pleasing, seeking approval and hanging on other's responses and judgements are some of the most draining and debilitating human experiences one could endure—a hell on Earth I would not wish on my enemy.

The opposite of this?
A liberation unlike anything else.

Constant Cravings And Toxic Traits

If we truly desire a peaceful and harmonious life, there has to be a point where we recognise any addiction to our abuse story and release it from our life.

Do our fears simply vanish over time? Do our desires and cravings to be praised and validated just disappear in a puff of smoke the moment our abusers are out of our lives? What about fear-based life choices? Do they just float off into the ether, never to be seen again?

The honest answer is the most confronting. And that's absolutely, categorically *no*. If left unchecked, our grooming-based cravings lead us to systematically attract one toxic person after another so we can recreate the same power dynamics we had with our abuser and re-enact our fear-based desires. That's how powerful these desires are. That's why we have to bring our full awareness to them and surrender them. This is one reason I advocate so strongly for 'doing the work' and healing our past. Do we really want to keep recreating toxic dynamics our whole lives?

In my story, I shared how I disclosed every part of my life to my abuser. If I displayed even a hint of independence or enjoyment from being around other people, he withheld his 'love' and immediately became cold and distant. His approval meant everything to me, so when he withheld it, it felt like death.

What did this do? It kept me even more controlled by my fear.

Never forget that the goal for these people is ultimate control. If we're constantly looking for a way out, they've failed in their mission. My abuser wanted me completely under his spell and craving his attention so he could withdraw it whenever he needed to. This is how grooming works. Why is this important? Because during my healing period, I became acutely aware of my desire for this particular type of 'attention'. My addiction compelled me to attract friends and partners who emulated this. So, without knowing it, I was subconsciously seeking a groomer. Due to years of meticulous programming, *I wanted to be groomed*. My unhealed desires were that strong.

This was a very uncomfortable realisation.

I had to get brutally honest with myself if I wanted to attract a different kind of person into my life, rather than the same old abusive dynamic I'd known. If I was getting to know someone new, I had to ask myself:

- What part of this relationship do I crave the most? And why? (Is it when I'm the focus of their attention? Is it only when we have sex? Is it when I'm giving them things?)
- Do I have certain desires for attention that feel like they can never be met?
- Do I act the same way around this person as I previously did? (Submissive, shy, dominated)
- Does this person share similar characteristics or behaviours? (Personality, looks, mannerisms, beliefs)

These questions helped me see something in a relationship I may have never noticed before, and when I made this discovery, it was *huge*. I learned at this particular time in my healing that I'd manifested a groomer in practically all of my close relationships. While not all of them were outwardly abusive, they all had one thing in common—they enabled me to give my power away. If you've recreated a toxic dynamic in your life, it's important to become aware of whether you're drawn to any particular aspects of that relationship. This is where the big lessons are. We cannot stop creating a toxic dynamic if we're unclear about what that dynamic looks like.

I encourage you to stop at this point and reflect on how you show up in each relationship in your life. Are there any areas where you are giving your power away?

Lower Your Abuse Threshold, Raise Your Vibe

You did not come this far, to just come this far.

Becoming aware of our deeper, more subconscious thoughts can be deeply shocking and confronting. I know when I came to the realisation I was attracted to certain situations, it was a bitter pill to swallow. How was my conditioning so strong that I was recreating abusive dynamics a decade later? The greater truth about all of this is once we become aware, things start to change for the better.

Why did it take so long before I realised this was toxic?

Let's examine it.

It's well known that traumatised people have a high threshold for abuse. We can reach a level nine or ten before we register any threat or attack. The key word here being 'register'. It's why we tolerate bad behaviour and it's paramount in understanding why many of us end up in abusive friendships and relationships. To put it simply, we're wired differently. We've been trained to never speak up, confront or defend ourselves, so someone being outwardly disrespectful to us won't always set off alarm bells. Our abuse bar is set so high that rude or derogatory behaviour can feel normal. It often takes something quite extreme to break through our threshold and catapult us into action. This is why people who have been abused can sometimes seem erratic. They've gone from being fast asleep to wide awake in the blink of an eye, by which time the metaphorical house is already on fire. They now go into fight or flight to escape their current situation.

When I realised this, I became paranoid and formed a reliance on others to see what I couldn't. I took anyone else's advice over my own because I thought I had to protect myself from my incapability.

As you can imagine, I created unhealthy and co-dependent relationships. I couldn't remove myself from a toxic dynamic because I didn't even recognise it was toxic in the first place. I needed a better system.

When I was getting to know and interacting with new people, I asked myself these questions:
- Do I feel this person cares about me?
- Does this person show any tenderness towards me?
- Are they dismissive towards of my thoughts and feelings?

- Do I feel comfortable around them?
- Did they help me love myself?
- Do they steer me away from unhealthy behaviours?
- Is there balanced receiving to my giving?

By shifting the focus away from detecting ill intent, and towards detecting care, I slowly cultivated more discernment. This became my benchmark for working out if a relationship was toxic or not.

In the early days of a healing journey, awareness can be the most important and powerful tool we have. I know for myself that even though I couldn't feel it, I would conceptualise it and choose to believe it because I resonated with it. It felt truthful. I could identify these concepts in Wave 2 within my own life. It became so black and white, so obvious to me, that I was attracting all these things. I realised a better way must be possible and that one day I would be so healed that these characters would simply stop appearing in my life.

Flashbacks, Memories And Letting It All Go

Nothing can 'come in' to your body anymore without your permission. It can only 'go out'. It's time to release.

We've discussed the deeper layers of trauma and how systematic it can become if left unchecked. Now let's switch gears and look at some of the more physical manifestations of healing trauma.

You'll probably notice as you reflect on the questions posed in this book that other memories may surface and pennies start to drop. This journey can be liberating, shattering and freeing—all in one! Trauma work is a lot like peeling an onion. The outside layer has to be peeled away before the deeper layers can emerge. When these repressed memories, and the associated beliefs and fears, resurface it can feel like a never-ending cycle of PTSD, but I can tell you, there is a method in the madness. We're working with innate intelligence here and, although it may not feel like it, we're receiving only what we're strong enough to see at the time.

In my opinion, PTSD (Post Traumatic Stress Disorder) could be called 'Unhealed Trauma Bubbling to the Surface'. I see it as the body needing to metaphorically release the trauma, and we need to pay attention. I've met a lot of people over the years who are absolutely terrified of their PTSD, as though it's a powerful outside force that takes them over. But in reality, PTSD can be a guide and a well-intentioned, loving friend. It's a powerful healing tool, provided it's harnessed properly and directed positively. Flashbacks and intense feelings are never there to hurt us. The pain we feel is simply stored and trapped distress that our bodies have been harbouring until it's safe to release. It feels painful when it comes out of us because the event that created it was painful. It hurts because the experience *did* hurt. A flashback, like dissociative behaviour (more on that later), is a gift that allows the unwanted to percolate to the top and be released from our bodies *forever*.

METAMORPHOSIS

Thought Forms And Emotional Flashbacks

*I have nothing to be afraid of at this moment.
Memories, yet painful, are harmless.*

Flashbacks aren't restricted to just images. They can come in the form of repetitive thoughts, too. If we experience looping thoughts, it can mean we're not taking enough time for ourselves. We may need to simply stop for a moment, sit with our trauma and see what it has to say. Looping flashbacks are like a neon sign from our subconscious, trying to draw our attention to where it needs to be.

When we experience prolonged periods of intense and debilitating fear, our bodies take on the burden of processing it, which takes a significant toll. Unfortunately, these emotions don't just disappear into the ether. They become deeply ingrained in the cellular memory of our bodies. Over time, it requires increasing amounts of energy to keep them all down. So, what can happen is they resurface as *emotional flashbacks*.

Emotional flashbacks can arise at any time, even while doing the most mundane, everyday activities. You could be driving down the street and suddenly be gripped by panic and fear, even though you're not in danger and nothing around you is triggering these feelings. Does this mean you've suddenly developed a phobia of driving? Probably not. It's more likely you're experiencing an emotional flashback.

Other common emotional flashbacks can include despondency, grief, anger and dissociation. It can be unsettling to experience these at first, but it's actually a good thing because it means the trapped emotions are resurfacing for release. Your body stored these emotions because you were unable to express them safely in the past. It's now time to allow your body to do what it needs to do.

It's important to recognise the incredible power of our own thoughts and begin to take responsibility for everything we think. This includes the present, the future and the past. Each memory can serve as a *golden key to our freedom*, with valuable information that can aid us in our healing process. Tuning into these memories, and acknowledging their significance as we release them, creates a gateway to healing and personal growth.

Here's an exercise I used to process my flashbacks and stop them from being repetitive:

1. Stop what you're doing and bring your attention to your breath.
2. Take a notebook and write down everything your memory is presenting to you. This doesn't have to be clear or structured, a simple stream of consciousness is fine (e.g., *I'm walking into a room wearing a red top and I see a big poster on the wall*).
3. Sit with the feeling in your body and notice how you react. Have you stopped breathing? Do you feel tense? Do you feel any other sensations in your body? Is this a familiar feeling or a new feeling?
4. Take another deep breath and stay with the feeling.
5. Are there any images surfacing? What feelings are arising? What other memories are coming up? Do you hear anything?

6. Now ask yourself this powerful question:
'Why am I being led to this memory?'

I recommend repeating these steps until the information held within the flashback becomes clear. We're never shown something for no reason, and when we take the time to integrate and release, the flashbacks often subside. If we allow ourselves to be constantly chased around by flashbacks, we only prolong the healing process. Remember, every point of our healing journey offers a choice. It's up to us to decide when to summon our strength and delve deep. It's easy to be drawn into ruminating on the past and all the bad things that happened. I've been there, and I understand how strong that pull can be. But having the discipline to move through these trapped memories and clear them is absolutely worth the effort.

One More Thing About Looping Flashbacks

There's no experience I fear when it comes from within my body.

If you had the option to stop having flashbacks completely, would you take it? Surprisingly, some of us may say no. That's because we either think it's impossible to let go, or on some level we can't imagine life without them. This is an example of attachment, or even addiction, to our trauma story. Complete honesty means considering whether we're allowing flashbacks to loop because we have some addiction to being scared or bullied by them. Once again, this comes back to being controlled. Releasing our co-dependency and controlling personalities also heals our dependency to being controlled. Giving our power away to flashbacks and not taking responsibility for them is allowing them to rule our lives once more.

When I share the controversial opinion that some people are choosing to be controlled by their PTSD and flashbacks, I often get the same response.

'But they are uncontrollable, and they run my life!'
I disagree.

I believe PTSD is our body's desperate attempt to communicate with us. When we have the right tools, and we apply ourselves completely, we can transmute all PTSD. I have demonstrated this over and over.

Here are some questions to gauge whether you could be addicted to your own trauma story. I encourage you to think deeply about these and answer honestly and without self-judgement:
- How would I feel if someone gave me the opportunity to never again feel pain or suffering when thinking about the past? Does it make me hesitant? Afraid of the loss? Or happy and relieved?
- If I could never speak about my past again, how would this change the way I show up in the world?
- Do I think about my pain and suffering when other people are sharing theirs? Do I want to compare stories or demonstrate that mine is worse?

- If I was given the opportunity to feel completely whole and healed, where I barely thought about my past at all, would I take it? How does my body feel about this?

For me, identifying with my old, wounded story helped me understand the reality of my situation. It didn't serve me to think I was healed because it simply wasn't the truth. I had a long journey ahead of me, and identifying and sharing my pain was necessary. But much later in my healing journey, I could release the attachment to my story because I no longer identified as a victim anymore. Releasing the victim gave me permission to take full responsibility for my flashbacks, my stories and my PTSD. I believe there's a point for all of us where we instinctively know we can release our attachment to our story, let go of the crutches and stand on our own two feet.

A Very Simple Truth

If I survived the actual abuse, I can survive the memory of it coming to the surface.

Before we move onto some of the more extreme trauma releases, I want to take a moment to remind you of a simple truth:

You survived the real thing.
The memory of it can't hurt you.
Memory is tricky.
And it's just that, a memory.

Memory is in the past.
It's not here in the room with you now.
In this moment, you're *not* being hurt. You're not being abused.

You are safe.

Let's Get Physical
(But Not Like That)

*In silence, all the secrets come out of hiding and
I'm shown the truth of my inner mind.*

When we discuss taking responsibility for our flashbacks and PTSD, what does this look like? How does this present itself? What can we expect when we allow our body to purge what it has been holding onto for so long?

When we start to dig deep into trauma, we may experience extra triggers, emotions and memories coming to the surface. In western medicine, I've been told this is PTSD and nothing can be done about it. But I believe this line of thinking discounts our body's innate wisdom and its ability to heal and restore us back to being whole. In fact, today, post-healing, I can categorically say that PTSD is just excess energy trying to come out of our body. The trick is working out how to expel it safely.

When my body, mind and spirit decided it was time to heal, it was as if everything wanted to be purged and I went through many visceral and even somatic responses. In hindsight, it makes sense that my body wanted to dispel and discharge that energy, but I wasn't prepared for it at the time. Until then, my trauma had been suppressed for almost ten years and, although highly dissociated, I lived a seemingly normal life. I had no idea just how much toxicity I carried until I began this process. Releasing it has restored an incredible amount of peace, health and wellbeing to my life.

Now that I've been through all these experiences, I'm sharing them here, so you have a point of reference if some or all of these symptoms arise. I wished I'd known these things could happen. It would have prevented a lot of extra fear and panic on my part. I want you to know that you are not alone. Embracing the process fully leads to a more peaceful life on the other side, I can assure you.

Here are some symptoms I experienced whilst releasing 'PTSD' from my body:

Head rushes: My head would feel warm, my heart rate would increase, and my breathing would become short and shallow, signalling the arrival of an emotional flashback or memory. What helped was focusing on long, deep breaths and reminding myself that the trauma was coming out of my body, not going in.

Reliving past pain: An 'abreaction' is when the body flashes back to the physical pain experienced at the time of abuse. Oftentimes when in meditation or as I was falling asleep, I'd feel a sharp pain in my abdomen, constriction in my chest or pain in a specific part of my body. This was my body literally re-enacting my experiences. The key is to remember it can't hurt you. It's simply coming up so it can be released forever.

PART TWO WAVE TWO

Memory flooding: I saw hundreds of images flash through my mind, and it always happened one of two ways. Breakneck speed, where I could barely distinguish one horrifying image from another, or as one particular scene being played out in minute detail, as if I was back there experiencing it again. During these moments, it felt like it would never stop, but all I needed to do was breathe deeply and thank it for releasing. The flooding of memories does slow down and stop. I used to think of it like fast forwarding an old VHS tape. It can't keep going indefinitely. Eventually, I reach the end of the tape.

Crying: I was never short of a tear. I cried throughout most of my two-year healing journey, and eventually, I had no shame about it. My healing was worth more than the judgments of others and I knew that to fully heal, I had to honour every tear that fell. I had a lot to cry about, and I let the cleansing release happen.

Sweating: Similar to crying, sweating is another way our body releases toxicity. It's essentially our body's way of crying. I often woke up drenched with sweat after a chaotic night's sleep. This was no light sheen, either. I looked like I'd come straight out of a swimming pool! I knew this was my traumatic past sweating itself out of every cell in my body, and I always felt lighter and energetically cleansed after an intense sweat session. The moral of the story? Never be afraid of what your body wants to serve up.

Shaking: Have you ever seen a dog shake itself off after a stressful interaction? Studies prove that animals who survive attacks in the wild literally shake off their trauma. Shaking is our body's natural way of dispelling negative charge and releasing shock from the system. I experienced jaw tremors, shaking hands and body trembles. At the time, I was afraid. I didn't know what was happening, but later I realised this was a natural way our body helps us out.

Panic attacks: In my experience, a panic attack is an overwhelming amount of energy trying to escape my body at once. It often coincided with negative and destructive thoughts—I held a belief at the time that something was drastically wrong with me. Most of my panic attacks happened right before going to sleep because I was terrified about what I was going to see in my dreams. Again, the body sometimes takes control, and we have to surrender to it. Panic attacks should never be feared. Yes, going through them can feel scary, but if we slow our breathing down, it brings instant reprieve and helps us regain control.

Night terrors: Night terrors are characterised by sudden episodes of complete panic, fear, disorientation and confusion. For me, it was as if my physical body knew where I was, but my mind was still caught up in a horrible memory or a dream. It could last anywhere up to a minute after waking. At the start of my healing, I experienced them every night. My anticipation of them triggered panic attacks because I was so terrified of what would emerge from my subconscious. I cannot begin to tell you how awful my dreams were—as bad, if not worse, than my abusive years. The good news is, as I continued to work on my healing and release, the night terrors subsided, and I started sleeping much more peacefully. This was also a positive indication of progress and healing.

Sleep paralysis: Similar to night terrors, sleep paralysis was a symptom I experienced more frequently earlier on. This involved waking up and being unable to move or speak, coupled with flashbacks of images, sounds and screaming voices. Over time, I became aware of contributing factors that increased the chances of sleep paralysis, including drinking alcohol, watching violent or scary movies and lack of sleep. What helped me was being very intentional and conscious of my environment and what I was consuming. As I healed, I became less affected by it and learned not to be so afraid of it. It happened so frequently early on that I just rode the wave because I knew the turbulence would pass.

Vertigo: One of the truly disorienting symptoms felt like the room was spinning at a thousand miles an hour, or like stepping off a dizzy whizzy ride in a playground. During the years I was abused, the cult members drugged me and spun me in circles while torturing or humiliating me. While they did this, they told me I was in different locations to confuse me and dissociate me further. I found that the vertigo was my body's attempt to clear the dissociation and disorientation from those experiences. The 'spinning' and 'out of control' sensations were coming out of my body as vertigo. What had come in, now went out.

Disorientation: Because of the dissociative nature of trauma, which I discuss in detail at the end of this Wave, it's easy to become disorientated post-abuse. It can happen when we're in social settings or even just in our own homes. For me, this was strongly connected to being moved around many different locations whilst drugged. Breathing slowly and strong affirmations helped anchor me in the present and confirm I was safe. As I healed, this symptom diminished.

We experience disorientation for two main reasons. The first is our minds are processing a memory of the past, so some aspect of us is still 'there' in that location. When we wake up in a different environment to what we were just experiencing in our dream or flashback, we feel disoriented. The second is that, in some circumstances, depending on our trauma, our minds are processing the emotional memory of 'confusion' itself. This was a huge part of my story because I was taken to so many places while drugged, and I was often confused about where I was.

Dealing with insomnia

For months during my healing crisis, I survived mostly on two to three hours of sleep each night. I dreaded going to bed and having to deal with the nightmares, flashbacks, and sleep paralysis. Even the thought of it caused me chronic anxiety and panic attacks. The worst of my flashbacks happened just as I was nodding off to sleep. My mind filled with words, images, and horrific memories that made me jolt straight out of bed. It was awful. I could manage the sleep paralysis, the night terrors, the disorientation and the nightmares, but the lack of sleep drove me to the edge of insanity. I knew if I didn't bring my sleep back into balance, I would fall right off that edge into crazy town. And once there, it would be very hard to come back.

I used these two techniques:

Meditation: I started practicing nightly meditation to ease me into a calm state of mind before bed. I drank herbal teas that supported relaxation and sleep. Chamomile, lavender, magnolia, passionflower and valerian are all sleep promoting options.

Reframing: I made a firm decision that I was no longer going to be bullied by these images. I consciously chose not to react to the disturbing visuals and memories that popped up just as I was falling asleep. Instead, I acknowledged them. *Ok, thank you for showing me but I need to sleep now.*

Whatever you experience, understand that it becomes less daunting over time. Imagine yourself carrying a backpack filled with rocks and every time you release a layer of trauma through a flashback or a nightmare, you get to drop one of them. You start to feel lighter, less burdened and freer. You're one step closer to being whole and at peace.

I'll Be Right There, Just Let Me Collect My Limbs

Dissociative behaviour reveals just how tenacious the human spirit is. If we were meant to give up easily, we could neve dissociate to the level some people have—it's about preservation of life.

Healing from trauma is not only complex, it can also feel frustratingly elusive. Your healing journey will be filled with twists and turns, surprises—good and bad—and moments of utter awe and inspiration. It's incredible to successfully heal oneself. It's something to be acknowledged and celebrated, not concealed in the shadows.

The truth is, schools and educational systems don't equip us with the necessary skills to heal ourselves from trauma, despite everyone being exposed to this universal experience to some degree or another. It's astounding that we aren't educated on this or given any strategies to confront and manage it ourselves. Consequently, we feel alone on our healing journey, believing we're the only ones going through this. We're not taught to reach out, express emotions or discuss our deepest, most painful memories. Instead, we believe we must bottle it up, push it down, keep everything inside and just cope with it on our own. This leads to an excessive amount of stagnant energy in our bodies that becomes expressed through addictions, controlling behaviour, abusive dynamics and, in the very worst cases, suicide, the ultimate 'evacuate' button for that trapped trauma energy. But all of it can be avoided.

Early on, I had to learn to be comfortable demonstrating boundless compassion towards myself. I also used a range of daily practices to safely channel the energy out of my body, dispersing the energy of guilt, shame and fear held deep within. A widely accepted view of PTSD is that it's a 'permanent disease of the mind'. I hold an alternative view that PTSD is our body reliving moments where we submitted our power in its entirety, perhaps from being forced to do something we were completely opposed to. In essence, we were removed and detached from our authentic self. In this way, we exhibit symptoms of PTSD not only from what we did, but because our authentic self is struggling to live with the part of ourselves that did it.

Abusers know the pinnacle of their control over us is when they don't even have to do the dirty work themselves. This happens when we start to perpetuate our own abuse, or we become an abuser ourselves.

Now, before we dive deeper into this delicate topic, I

want you to remember one of the key messages from the start of Wave 1. You are the victim of abuse, and you were manipulated and coerced into participating in activities against your will. No one is blaming you for that. We're simply unpacking that victimised aspect of ourselves and taking charge to restore our agency and personal freedom.

One of the key trauma responses we need to understand if we want to lessen the symptoms of PTSD is dissociative behaviour. Dissociative behaviour involves a disconnection or dissociation between our thoughts, emotions, perceptions and identity. In other words, when we're experiencing dissociation, we may feel as if we're not fully present in our surroundings or in our own body. It occurs when the external environment becomes so violent or overwhelmingly stressful that we, as the victim, mentally 'check out'. It's actually quite a valuable coping mechanism. In time, you may come to appreciate the protective function of dissociation. It's one way our body steps in to shield our minds from harm.

Now, at this point in the book, you may feel a little overwhelmed. I mean, why are we left with such an enormous task of healing and discovery? I completely understand. So far, we've discussed fear, false beliefs, fear-based decision processes, toxic friendships and relationships, attracting abusive dynamics towards us, and the list goes on. While we may want to pretend we can just cope our way through life, that's not going to help us. Our trauma is not going anywhere until we take charge and act. So why not take radical responsibility for, not just your healing journey, but your entire self?

Dissociation can divide us into multiple parts, and each part has learned to deal with different types of abuse. This masterful intelligence has kept us safe, but now we need to go deep into the mysterious world of dissociative behaviour and its symptoms. We must reclaim the lost aspects of ourselves.

Dissociation: a mental escape when physical escape isn't possible

As discussed above, dissociation is a coping mechanism that activates when we find ourselves in highly stressful, painful or traumatic situations. We can retreat into safety by disconnecting from everything around us, including our thoughts, feelings and sense of identity. Because we can only handle so much pain, our brain compartmentalises the abuse so as not to overwhelm us. I liken it to carrying grocery bags—putting all the weight in one bag probably results in a break, but distributing it across several bags makes it easier to manage. When you think about it, it's quite remarkable that our brain has the capacity to protect us in this way. Without the ability to dissociate during abuse, we would have experienced all the pain being inflicted on us at once and, like the grocery bag, we would have broken.

Dissociation can range from mild, such as fading in and out of reality (what I refer to as ghosting), to severe forms where multiple personalities are created to deal with the trauma. These personalities may have distinct names, behaviours, speech patterns, tones of voice, and even different blood pressure readings. During my years of abuse, I would lose track of time completely, with no recollection of the intervening hours. For me, it felt like jumping from 8.00 pm to 1.00 am in the blink of an eye.

In situations like these, dissociation really is the ultimate gift.

PART TWO WAVE TWO

*We reach our threshold of pain and in that moment, we split into two, then three, then four, and so on. We have never ending silos for pain which demonstrate our will to survive. If our will to survive is this strong, it implies an immeasurable ability to heal as well.
The amount of energy to preserve life is the same energy to heal life.*

Some common signs of dissociative behaviour include:
- Feeling detached from your surroundings, zoning out or appearing vacant
- Losing time, where hours, days can feel like they have passed in an instant
- Difficulty concentrating or focusing
- Feeling like you're not 'in your body'
- Feeling restless and constantly wanting to be somewhere else
- Always thinking of the next thing to do or say to avoid the present moment
- Thinking of suiciding or feeling depressed, anxious and alone
- Non-stop 'doing' combined with anxiousness or discomfort
- Changing clothes often and not feeling settled in your skin

All these behaviours can keep the fight-or-flight part of our brain firing, which releases the stress hormone cortisol and therefore triggers dissociation. If we feel uncomfortable, we may dissociate more frequently, so we need to analyse why our current environment is unsettling. Even seemingly minor triggers, such as a passing comment or a certain facial expression, can result in an immediate dissociative response. It can happen in subtle and involuntary ways, where we may not realise we've dissociated because ninety per cent of us is still present. In these moments, the true self, with its full range of emotions and responses, steps aside, and the facade takes over. Dissociation in this mild form is not dangerous. It's just representative of an unhealed aspect of ourselves and once we become aware we could be dissociating, we can become more attuned to it.

Depersonalisation: I'm completely detached from what's happening around me

Depersonalisation is where you feel completely outside of yourself, like you're observing your actions from a distance, rather than experiencing them from inside your own body. This can feel like:
- Floating in the air above yourself in a complete out-of-body experience
- The sense that your limbs are detached or distorted—perhaps they feel like they're in another room
- Feeling like you're in a dream, rather than experiencing reality
- Inability to form speech
- Seeing objects as larger or smaller than they are

Many times in my life, I couldn't feel a certain part of my body. I was convinced my body parts had been separated and were in different multiple locations.

Derealisation: I don't know what's real anymore

Derealisation is the feeling of being so alienated from your surroundings and the world that nothing makes sense. The world feels unreal or distorted, almost like being in a dream or a movie. Everything is disconnected. The difference between derealisation and depersonalisation is that depersonalisation feels like being outside of yourself, whereas derealisation feels like the world around you isn't real.

An example of derealisation in my life was when I'd be walking along the beach then suddenly have no idea how to walk. I couldn't understand what the sand was, and I'd think:

- *What is this granular substance under my feet and why am I not falling straight through it?* (The sand.)
- *Why is there blue paint above my head?* (The sky.)
- *What are the white substances in the blue paint?* (The clouds.)
- *What are these creatures with two arms and two legs doing?* (People.)

My tips for managing the three Ds

Heal the dissociation and watch your life blossom before your eyes.

If all your pain has been carefully placed in the custody of the most intelligent aspect of your being, can you appreciate how profound and beautiful that is? This part of you has stored and managed aspects of your abuse and knows just how much to reveal at any given moment so you can safely manage your healing. Dissociative behaviour is exactly this, the management of our abuse by the higher intelligence that lives within us all. While we can be grateful to this part of ourselves for gradually exposing our painful memories to avoid overwhelming us, it still doesn't make for the easiest ride.

Experiencing these dissociative conditions firsthand can be terrifying, but we can do things to manage it. For example, when I understood derealisation is fuelled by fear, I stopped being afraid of when I would experience it. Instead, I found it helpful to expect to de-realise during dissociation. Simply by expecting it, I could reduce the fear of it and lower the chances of it happening.

Unfortunately, this doesn't stop the frustration!

So many times, I found myself frustrated by my various dissociative conditions and had to remind myself why they were there. My dissociative superpowers were protective mechanisms there to help me. They may be frustrating to deal with, but they saved my life and my sanity back then. However, now I had to release the energy being consumed by keeping these protective mechanisms in place. Imagine if I could let my mind finally rest? What would it feel like to claim back that energy for myself?

I wanted to understand exactly how I could reduce my dissociative behaviours and reintegrate to become fully present in my life. I discovered the following:

Watch your triggers
When we experience cortisol dumps (the hormone produced during extreme stress), this can cause us to easily disassociate. To counteract this, I became hyper aware of my stress levels and monitored the environments, places and people I reacted to. I took note of anything that made me uneasy, scared, nervous, overwhelmed or uncomfortable and avoided these situations wherever possible. Remember that dissociation is a defensive mechanism. Any environment that makes you feel defensive or puts

you on edge could trigger it. It helps to be conscious about this process. Really tune in and get honest with it. It's not unusual to find that a family member, close friend or even a partner is triggering some of your dissociation.

Breathe and receive

When I dissociate, I tend to hold my breath. To prevent dissociation, I focused on taking slow, deep, deliberate breaths to stay grounded and present in the moment. I told myself to 'breathe and receive', whether I was receiving a loving touch, a bowl of delicious food or even just the gentle breeze on my skin. Dissociation is essentially an avoidance or rejection of a current experience, so 'breathe and receive' helped me relax into the present moment and what was happening within and around me.

During depersonalisation, have conscious conversations

I asked myself questions to bring present awareness back to my body, and I'd ask them in a playful way—and with a smile—to diffuse the anxiety that depersonalising caused me.

Here's a typical conversation I had during this time:

Q: Where is my head?
A: *Well, it's on the ceiling ... (the sensation that is)*

Q: Where are my legs?
A: *Well, one of them is here, but the other is in the corner of the room ...*

Then, I'd bring present awareness to my current environment to bring my body back into the room.

Q: What can I feel around me?
A: *I can feel the pillow under my head, the material on my skin.*

Q: What is the temperature right now?
A: *The temperature is cold because it is winter, and the windows are open.*

Q: What does the material feel like on my skin?
A: *The material is fleecy and warm. I can feel the cotton on my skin.*

I continued this exercise until I was embodied once again, while saying:

I call my body back home.
I ask for help bringing my body back to centre and feeling whole.
I am safe, I am home. I am safe, I am home.

These two exercises brought constant attention to the behaviour, so the effects of it became less over time. It's important to approach them with deep compassion towards yourself. It's the key to achieving personal freedom.

We cannot and should not underestimate the impact of abuse on our bodies and minds. During those times, dissociation was our life raft, our ally and the only way we could have survived. Some of us may have dissociated for years, meaning our body became masterful at doing it.

PART TWO WAVE TWO

The Four Seasons of Trauma

Clock hands move forward, not backwards.

It's normal for trauma, fears and stories to rise up when we're entrenched in the healing process. But understanding and accepting the impermanence of everything allows us to stay strong and composed. I like to think of the phases of healing as seasons. We have to go through them, but they don't last forever.

When the most intense aspects of my trauma surfaced, it felt like a harsh and relentless winter. My emotions were raw, my outlook was bleak, and I was drowning in a sea of my own tears. All I wanted was a break and for the sun to come out. But the thing about winter is, although it feels like it will never end when you're in the thick of it, spring always comes around, bringing growth, new opportunities and fresh perspectives.

In spring, you might feel hope creeping back into your heart and perhaps even gratitude for the heavy release of grief and pain. You can plant the seeds of a new life you envision for yourself and, in summer, you begin to see them thrive.

During summer, you might find you don't have many flashbacks and you feel like the world might just be okay. The trauma isn't as much of a foreboding presence during summer. Life is easier and more peaceful.

Enjoy the respite and, when autumn arrives, you'll naturally feel the need to retreat, reflect and be on your own. This phase is a perfect time to process the events of summer and reflect on your growth. You turn inward and allow what no longer serves you to just gracefully fall away.

Be patient with yourself

In the early stages of my trauma release, I could experience all four seasons in a week, or sometimes even a day. But now, there's much longer between each season and I rarely feel the intense 'winter' months anymore. In fact, my life resembles summer most of the time—with the occasional 'weather warning' thrown in for good measure!

This is why it is important not to label our healing or attach a timeline to it. Things occur when they need to. Trust that learning, enlightenment and growth are around every corner. If I can offer any wisdom with these ups and downs, it's this:
- Try to have no attachment to the outcome
- Enjoy the moments when you feel good
- Don't assume the worst is over
- Take each day as it comes

In Waves 3 and 4, we dive deep into how to cultivate self-worth and self-respect, two key ingredients that bring in the new, healed version of ourselves and put an end to fear-based co-dependency forever.

Wave 3

Positive Shifts, Empowerment And Self-Worth

To give another so much power, to enthrone them in your mind, is an insult to your own greatness.

Up until this point, we've uncovered many aspects of ourselves, revealed the patterns and behaviours holding us back and exposed the fears that have been running the show. But what do we now do with these newfound realisations? And how do we integrate them to start bringing in our new self?

We do it through the simple but powerful act of letting go.

Wave 3 is a psychological purging of everything we're holding onto that no longer serves us. Here, we discuss how abuse has stifled our expression and forced us to assume a guilty and shame-filled position in life, rather than a free and loving one. We look at the mental prison we could be living in as a result of our traumatic pasts.

Here's the catch.

To move forward, we must be totally honest about the restrictive behaviours that could be running on autopilot, and approach this examination with honesty, openness, and self-compassion. If we're unaware of the things holding us back, and how they got there in the first place, how can we expect to release them? How can we prosper when patterns and behaviours from the past are keeping us stuck today?

The answer is, we can't.

In Wave 3, I present you one paradigm shift after another, and a completely new way to think about and release your trauma to create space for what is more truthful and loving. We discuss your internal world and what makes you tick, in particular:
- Cultivating self-worth
- Relinquishing your desire to control
- Recalibrating the meaning of Right and Wrong
- Recognising what is yours and what is not
- How your thoughts can be your own worst enemy
- Surrendering the victim mentality and embracing all that you are
- How patterns of abuse creep into today's world—and how to free yourself of them

When I started fully reclaiming my self-worth, it was as if I'd unlocked a new level of personal power I never knew existed. Prioritising my own needs in a healthy way and experiencing genuine comfort, happiness and inner peace was a revelation. I'd always understood self-love as an elusive and abstract concept. I never expected I could embody it. When I discovered this superpower, I couldn't believe what I'd found. But the thing is, this wasn't a new power at all. It was just buried under layers of self-judgement, suffering, guilt and shame. I share the simple methods that helped me unearth it, cultivate self-love and self-worth and show up in the world more confidently and in my power.

With this Wave, I invite you to look through a different lens and realise that some of the closely guarded behaviours you exhibit today, and some relationships you hold so closely to your heart, may just need to go.

Are you ready to discover the new you?

Where Did My Self Worth Go?
(And How Can I Get It Back)

*Keep breaking through, keep moving forward.
Light is at the end of the tunnel.*

Self-worth is, in its most simple definition, a sense of one's own value as a human being.

Sounds simple enough, right?

So, how do we get to a place of valuing ourselves and believing we deserve respect when we've spent so many years being diminished and devalued? Every month my abuse went on, my self-worth diminished, and compliance and obedience took its place. When I examined this more closely, I saw that self-worth and slavery existed at opposite ends of the spectrum and self-worth couldn't coexist with a slavery mindset. When we have a sense of self-worth, we respect our own feelings, decisions and emotions.

Imagine you've been listening to a radio producing constant static for years, making it difficult to hear anything clearly. Then, one day you suddenly tune into a brand-new frequency! The crackly radio station has transformed into a high-quality broadcast with crystal clear clarity. This is what it can feel like to go through the process of healing and discover your own inner strength. Interestingly, the journey itself helped me reach this point. If I had bypassed the work or ignored the tough moments when they arose, I could never have reached this point of growth. By doing the work, learning from my mistakes and persisting through the tough moments, I was able to heal my trauma and gain my resilience and strength.

For example, if I felt a strong urge to cry or get angry, or if I felt rage percolating inside me, I showed up for myself and took the time to acknowledge and process those emotions rather than bottling them up. I knew they weren't there to harm me, but to help me grow and heal. I admit it wasn't always easy to deal with them. Many were uncomfortable and painful, but I knew it was worth it.

In contrast, when we allow our traumatic stories, narratives, and emotions to constantly loop in our minds, we give them power over us. We choose to be dominated by these thoughts and feelings, rather than acknowledging them and allowing them to exist for what they are. This can be a challenging cycle to break, especially if we've carried these burdens for a long time. However, we can change our relationship with these experiences.

There is no honour in coping, battling or doing it tough.
This is not self-love. This is self-victimisation.

Some of us centre our entire identity around our pain and suffering. Some of us descend into deep depression and anxiety and stop fully engaging with our lives, and some of us use our trauma as a protective shield. We harden ourselves against the world and everyone in it. We become cold and distant to avoid feeling our deepest feelings. Although we feel strong and tough wearing this suit of armour, sooner or later, it needs to come off.

I ask you this question. What resonates more truthfully for you when it comes to self-worth?

- To honour and sit with your feelings and emotions, even if it makes you feel upset, angry and frustrated?
- To allow past stories and pain to loop continuously in your mind and control you?
- To shield yourself forever and shut yourself off from the world so you don't get hurt again?

Self-love is not a false display of bravery to the world. It's a softening into how you feel in your body and the flourishing of a deeply personal relationship with yourself. It's being able to rely one hundred per cent on your inner guidance and trust it with such certainty, you never doubt your decisions or choices. When you have this connection, you'll never concede your sovereignty or individuality again.

Through the exercises and questions I've shared with you, I rebuilt my confidence and cultivated discernment to where I now trust and respect myself implicitly. Being able to navigate life's challenges calmly and confidently is a truly amazing place to be.

Remember, no matter how much static or noise we may encounter in life, there is always the possibility of tuning in to the crystal-clear broadcast of our inner power and discovering our own path to healing and growth.

METAMORPHOSIS

Taming Your Inner Control Freak

I'm tired of sacrificing myself, sacrificing how I feel for the needs of others.

As we start reconnecting with our true selves, we begin to notice all the ways control has been a major theme in our lives. Now, I'm not talking about overt control, which is visible, apparent and openly displayed. I'm talking about something much more insidious—covert control. Let's break this down.

As survivors, someone in our past has exercised control over us and we were unable to do anything about it. If we tried to advocate for ourselves, we were most likely punished in horrible ways. We learned that healthy and natural behaviours, such as expressing our feelings or displaying any type of agency over ourselves or our surroundings, were unacceptable. This alone can have a systemic and devastating impact on our life because we learn to direct these feelings inwards and express ourselves covertly, rather than openly and directly. It wasn't something we set out to do and become obsessive about. We simply needed our world to be a certain way to avoid being hurt again. We did it to feel safe.

Control isn't the same as freedom

Covert control gave me a false sense of safety and security. I reasoned that if I had control of everything

around me post-abuse, I'd be able to reclaim my power. It was a well-intended goal, but I was going about it in a toxic way that I would later need to heal from. This looked like:
- Hiding my emotions and not being honest with others
- Refusing to communicate my expectations, yet being disappointed when they weren't met
- Being overly generous with time, money and gifts
- Staying in toxic relationships and being victimised further
- Displaying erratic, overly emotional, hyper-affectionate behaviours
- Leading conversations toward a certain outcome in personal relationships
- Intentionally behaving in a way that caused worry or concern (e.g., not answering the phone)
- Not expressing my feelings for fear of being abandoned

Such patterns can be deeply ingrained and buried in our subconscious, just like the other negative learned behaviours and beliefs we've developed over time. Predetermining outcomes, being fearful when they don't go our way, and needing things to be exactly how we see them in our minds is an exhausting way to live. They do nothing to affirm our faith and belief in ourselves. The truth is, we can't control anyone in this world but ourselves, and the quicker we accept this, the quicker deep healing can take place. Imagine how freeing it would be to release that tightly held leash on everything and everyone around us? To surrender and allow life to unfold naturally without managing every outcome, relationship or circumstance?

Well, I can tell you how it feels. It's freaking terrifying!

At first.

METAMORPHOSIS

When I started to break down my control walls, I cried for months. It was extremely intimidating to just allow things to happen. The term 'go with the flow' was not in my vocabulary! My fear and control were obsessive because I thought I *needed* to be in control, not only to get a particular outcome, but to survive. With time and practise, I learned to surrender to life, to have faith and, most importantly, trust. When I stopped trying to control everything around me, my nervous system unlocked and the fight-or-flight part of my brain could finally rest. It was as if my body exhaled for the first time in years. I started to let go.

So, how do you surrender control?
It starts with being able to recognise and acknowledge it.

I asked myself these questions so I could identify when my inner control freak was attempting to take over:
- Do I feel uneasy when things don't go my way? Do I lose interest in the conversation or feel bothered or irritated?
- Do I handle change poorly? If a planned event gets changed last minute, how does it make me feel?
- What am I doing in excess for my friends or family that isn't being reciprocated?
  Am I doing the jobs no one else wants to do? Cooking more than anyone else? Always paying for things when we go out?
- Am I constantly giving people affection? Why do I think I'm so affectionate?
- Do I get irritated with people easily and find it difficult to communicate openly with them?
- Do I find myself trying to manage or fix everything around me? (This is particularly unhealthy for women as it shifts us out of feminine energy and into a masculine role)

- Do I censor myself instead of speaking the entire truth to avoid confrontation? (Avoidance is also control)

Do you see the theme? If you answered yes to all these questions, you have a strong attachment to a particular outcome.

When we drop any need for control and apply a cognitive frame to trust and surrender, we find ourselves reacting to situations differently. If things don't go our way, we can allow it and trust that it'll still be fine. If plans change, we learn to roll with it. And if friends or family don't reciprocate our generosity? We learn to make things more balanced in the future.

Covert control is an understandable by-product of being abused. We never intended to control our world. We did this to survive. Our goal now is to release our iron grip on outcomes and embrace the flow of life. By allowing what is and detaching from any outcome, we automatically place ourselves in a more loving, trusting and peaceful place.

Releasing covert control and stepping into trust is a journey, not an instant fix. It can take years to unravel this, and it requires continuous awareness and self-compassion. For many, covert control could be a lifelong habit, so it makes sense that it takes time to release and rewire.

METAMORPHOSIS

Facing The Bully Within

We get so caught up in the right and the wrong that we miss the blessing in front of us.

One day, part way through this healing journey, I had an epiphany.
I was allowing my own thoughts to bully me. And I'd been doing it for a very long time.

Looking back through my personal journal entries, I could see I'd been stuck in this battle for nearly a decade. I was filtering my life choices and decisions through the lens of what I thought was 'right and wrong', but I'd created such high expectations of myself that I was judging my behaviour way too harshly. I'd created a construct of 'criminal' and 'punisher' within me, where two facets of my personality were in constant opposition. One was doing the bullying, and one was receiving it. I was constantly at war with myself.

As I mentioned in Wave 2, my people-pleasing was extreme. I told myself I could never disappoint people or make a mistake. However, looking back, I can see I was attracting exactly the type of people who punished me for making mistakes. I became aware that I was existing through an overzealous framework of right or wrong which was perpetuating separateness and keeping me enslaved by the 'bully' and 'victim' aspects of my mind. My harmful inner dialogue was preventing me from trusting my own decisions, so I would seek approval or 'go-ahead' from others and constantly give my power away.

I needed to reclaim my self-respect and put my inner bully back in its place.
I started with awareness.

Survivors often have issues trusting our gut instincts because, as discussed in Wave 1, our internal compass was commandeered by an abuser. Our will power is linked strongly to our instinct, so abuse can dismantle this very effectively. But the wonderful thing is, once we start to heal, our intuition begins to come back to us.

Full disclosure, the initial stages of trusting myself weren't easy. I was groomed to be completely reliant on the instructions of others, and going against that was a highly punishable offence. I formed such a strong reliance on the opinions and approval of others that stopping cold turkey felt like weaning myself off a powerful drug. I went through an 'opinions of others' detox and experienced intense periods of anxiety where I felt the 'fear of making a mistake' quite literally coming out of my body. What made it worse was other people telling me directly that I had no ability to discern right from wrong because of my abuse. To a degree they were correct, but also, *how dare they!* I was ready to start experimenting with life and if that meant making mistakes for the first time ever, so be it.
I started to have stronger opinions and feelings about what was right for me and what I wanted to do, as opposed to what others thought I should. I could feel a level of independence forming and, in some way, I felt like an adult for the first time in my life. I felt my power returning. This didn't mean I was seeking to become a hyper-independent

woman who didn't need anything from anyone, but I was more in touch with my own instincts. I could determine for the first time in my life what felt loving and right for me. As my confidence grew, I experimented with larger decisions and even went through the daunting and uncomfortable experience of making up my own mind. I still felt the fear arise, but I reasoned that I'd never fully heal if I kept relying exclusively on other people for advice. For weeks, I trained myself to tune into my feelings first before asking any questions. I listened to my body's instinctual response and learned to be okay with making mistakes and not doing everything perfectly. I also learned to be okay with loved ones being disappointed in me and hearing things like 'I told you so'. Eventually, I got better at listening to my body and these days I trust my instincts one hundred per cent of the time. I released the idea of being 'absolutely perfect' and the addiction to other people's advice. I started living my life in perfect alignment to my own instinct.

What a blessing.

Creating Healthy Boundaries

We approach healers for two reasons.
To confirm a narrative of being a victim or to affirm
faith in our own ability to heal and be whole.

Abuse can haunt us for years, sometimes decades, of our lives, whether it's trauma from the actual abuse, or dealing with the fallout, memories, triggers and the ongoing impact it has on our lives.

Ask yourself:
- How many days do I spend thinking about my abuse? Or talking about it?
- How often do past abusive scenarios run through my mind?
- How much therapy and treatment have I undergone?
- How long has it been since the traumatic event happened?

Reflecting on these questions, we can see just how much we're focusing on our trauma story and unconsciously centring our life around it. No wonder it's difficult to be present or find peace. Who could possibly be at peace with memories haunting them every minute of the day? If we find ourselves stuck in a trauma loop, it may be because:
- We've developed a habit of talking about it every day
- We allow ourselves to feel triggered by life
- We're permanently trying to fix ourselves and move onto the next thing, rather than actually embodying what we learn

For me personally, there was a time in my healing journey where I felt I'd lost connection to reality and absolutely everything seemed to be about my healing. It totally consumed my life and I couldn't even hold a conversation about anything else. This didn't happen immediately, but built up over several months until, before I knew it, my trauma was centre stage and running the show. Again.

I had to cultivate more self-discipline so I could put healthy boundaries around my healing. This is how I did it:

- I noticed how often I wanted to talk about my trauma in conversations. If I felt the urge to do it, I stopped myself and intentionally observed my desire to speak.
- I began attentively listening to other people, rather than waiting for my turn to speak about my trauma.
- I journalled at a specific time each day to release mental tension and document any flashbacks. This gave me an outlet for the thoughts circling around in my head, and I could channel them more appropriately.
- Every time something triggered me, I got out my phone and made a note of it for later reference when I was journalling. I found that once I'd documented it, the energy of that image or memory dissipated.
- I remained conscious of my breathing and focused on long, steady breaths in and out.

These tips helped me stay present and created a proactive channel for my energy and obsession with my healing journey. Remember, this is not about suppressing our trauma. It's about managing it so it can be released. Everything we're doing here is to move us out of a victimised state and put us back in the driver's seat of our life. The more we actively manage and express our trauma in productive and supportive ways, the closer we come to integration and becoming whole again. Or, as I like to say, reach a deep sense of inner peace.

PART TWO WAVE THREE

No More Drama—Choosing Empowerment Over Victimhood

I asked myself 1,000 times why I experienced the worst abuse imaginable. Well, it's because at the time of abuse, I didn't know anything else was even possible. But now I know, and it gives me focus, drive and motivation.

Our bodies hold on to the memory of trauma, often as physical sensations or symptoms, but the way we think about our trauma changes everything. If we constantly replay traumatic events in our minds without releasing them, we become trapped in a cycle of re-experiencing the trauma over and over again. However, when we rethink our trauma, it can't loop in our minds and haunt us.

Now, I'm not suggesting you dismiss everything that's happened to you or deny your trauma's existence. Far from it. What I'm talking about is learning to understand that, as complex and formidable as your trauma is, it doesn't have to control your life anymore. It's about training your brain to relate to your trauma differently. It's about a simple shift in perspective.

I know that if you've been carrying this trauma with you for years, you're so intimately familiar with it that it's almost a loyal and dependable companion. It can feel impossible to think of it any other way.

A big shift came for me when I realised a confronting truth.
There is a certain appeal in staying a victim.

Victimhood wasn't just comfortable. It was inviting and seductive. It allowed me to indulge in my brokenness and avoid taking responsibility for my own actions. I could be dysfunctional in any way and people just had to cope with my erratic behaviour. I'm a victim, after all. And while true, having such a strong attachment to victimhood suppressed me. It kept me small and weak and believing I was powerless. For example, if I ever needed to make a decision, I asked everyone around me for their advice rather than connecting with my own. I constantly doubted myself and had no idea how to make a decision independently. Free will was a foreign concept to me and intuition had left the building a long time ago. In short, my inner guidance system was offline.

When I started shifting my perception and training my mind to relate to my trauma differently, I began to see something else. I was enabling myself.

It was uncomfortable to admit, but it was the truth. And radical self-honesty is often what's required when we're on a journey of healing. I wanted to make a clear distinction between being a victim and being empowered by asking myself these questions:

- Have I gravitated towards situations that kept me small and weak?
- Has being a victim ever provided me with benefits—perceived or tangible?
- How do those benefits show up in my life?
- Do I feel like I've handed over power or control of myself to someone else?

Surrendering the victim

One reason people shy away from trauma recovery is that it requires us to release the familiar so the *unfamiliar* can come in. For many people, the unknown is far scarier than the known, even if it means holding onto our victim story and with it, a paralysing level of pain. Our story may have become so fused with our identity we feel empty or hollow without it. This is a major factor preventing us from stepping fully into our power as an individual. The truth is, for most of us, an unhealthy co-dependency exists between us and our victim story, and it has allowed us to avoid our healing responsibilities in various ways. For example, say we're having serious relationship issues, but rather than address the underlying issues or work towards a resolution, we choose to abandon it and blame the past. In other words, relying on the 'excuse' is easier than doing the work.

So where do we go from here?

First, recognising we're addicted to our own suffering and, in some cases, absorbed in our trauma stories is nothing to be ashamed of. It takes courage, honesty and vulnerability to see. Second, if we really want to release the grip of our inner victim, we need to take radical responsibility.

Ask yourself these questions (honestly, and without judgement):
- If I was never allowed to talk about my trauma ever again, how would I feel?
- If someone could wave a magic wand to erase the memories, would I let them?
- If I could never suffer again from my abusive past, would I say yes?

- If I could have a loving, grounded partner who gives me nothing but unconditional love no matter what, would I accept them?
- How would I feel if I took one hundred per cent of the responsibility for the way my life is right now, without linking it to anything in the past?
- What if I felt healed and at peace from this moment on?

These questions are simply to gauge how attached you could be to your inner victim.

An important distinction

Let me emphasise that it's perfectly fine for you to reveal details about your past to anyone you're comfortable with. It's human nature to want to connect and reveal deeper layers of yourself as you're getting to know someone and forming relationships. But be mindful when sharing this information. Are you approaching it from a place of empowerment? Or victimhood?

The paradox of being a victim is we sustain the narrative ourselves. When we're aligning with victimhood, we're projecting a disempowered demeanour, one where something 'happened to us' and 'we are suffering' yet, in reality, we are often the ones perpetuating it. Inherently, our inner victim becomes self-perpetuating at every level.

Another thing.

If we choose to represent ourselves as a victim who cannot function in life, we're demeaning ourselves and doing the work of our abuser. And none of us want to do that. The key is to want our healing more than we desire the addiction to victimhood. When this happens, it is a game changer for life.

When I started detaching from my inner victim and my stories, I experienced, for the first time in my life, what it meant to be me. The real me, not the traumatised version who had been representing me for so many years. And you know what? It was like I was meeting myself for the first time. And what's even more surprising, I didn't hate the person I was meeting! For someone who had been at war with themselves for the past decade, this felt like a revolution. Once I got there, I knew there was no turning back. I knew I had to go the entire way.

I ask you, how willing are you to surrender your inner victim? How willing are you to take a leap of faith and discover who you truly are? This surrendering is where the magic truly happens. The part most people don't like is the walk between these two worlds. It is scary, yes. But trust me when I tell you, it's well worth it. Surrendering your inner victim is an acknowledgement that you're ready to step fully into your power and you're on your way to complete freedom and liberation.

METAMORPHOSIS

Releasing Disappointment Forever

The conditioning from abusers works best through a cognitive frame of guilt, shame or disappointment. If we drop this frame, there's nothing to hold the facade in place.

Disappointment: The negative emotion you feel when an outcome doesn't match up to your expectations.

'I am so disappointed in you.'

I heard this statement many times in my life, from my abusers, my previous romantic partners and even my former friends. For years, I believed I was a total disappointment who never did anything right. I lived much of my life walking on eggshells and, let me tell you, it was utterly exhausting! The fear of disappointing is one of the foundations of my grooming and is deeply rooted in my abuse. If I didn't comply in the exact way they wanted me to, it meant abandonment, isolation, or more abuse. So, I gave up any notion of what I considered right or wrong and adopted an attitude of never disappointing them instead. I forfeited my self-worth and inner guidance system. I forfeited my human right to say, 'No.' And I experienced too many abusive relationships and toxic friendships before I saw this and addressed it.

Having said that, disappointment is largely based on

beliefs. So, when we begin to recognise our own self-worth, we naturally become less bothered by the disappointment of others. What was once all tied in together can be unravelled pretty quickly.

To be free of expectations in the context of a relationship means you honour your own feelings more than you minimise your needs to please another. This is a great gift of self-love.

You can feel it without believing it

When a person makes a judgement that they're disappointed in us, we have two options. The first is to accept that judgement as truth and allow ourselves to feel like a disappointment. We may even create our own narrative to justify *why* we're such a disappointment. The second option is to feel our *reaction* to 'being a disappointment' and then let it go. That's it. Don't allow it to penetrate our thoughts or energy. If we don't consent to somebody else's judgement affecting us, we simply don't identify with it. The same applies to any other emotion being projected onto us.

Remember, what other people think of you is none of your business. Adopting this attitude is a liberating way to stop absorbing the negative and projected beliefs of others. Here are some steps to take next time someone makes a judgement toward you:
1. Close your eyes and feel how you reacted to this judgement. Do you feel anger, sadness, confusion, anxiety, guilt, shame, blame, disappointment?
2. Now go even deeper. What physical sensations do you feel (e.g., hot, cold, etc.)? Does the emotion intensify now you're focusing on it?

3. Trying hard to reserve judgement, just focus on the feeling and stay out of the story. Just feel it until it melts into your body
4. Say to yourself, I do not consent to your blame/shame/disappointment
5. Now open your eyes

If you noticed there's no story you're aligning to—congratulations, you've successfully defended yourself against projection and judgement. This is true self-worth. Remember, there's no end goal when it comes to self-worth. It's a continuous journey that requires awareness, consciousness and self-compassion. Over time, we notice improvements and changes that are lifelong. It just takes courage to begin the change within.

Be Mindful Of The Double Life

A big epiphany during my healing journey was the realisation I'd been living a double life, year in, year out, with every single person who crossed my path. In one reality, I felt like my authentic and integrated self, but in the other, I was secretive, dissociated and afraid. The reason for this, no surprise, goes back to my abuse. When I was young, my normal life revolved around my family, friends and going to university. In this version of my life, I felt like myself. No one else was in control of me. I was free. But I also had another 'secret' life where I was embroiled in an abusive relationship with my tutor. In this world, the overwhelming feeling was of secrecy and oppression.

For years, I moved between the two worlds like a chameleon. The person I was in one world was drastically different to who I was in the other, and I could switch between them in seconds. I'd created a complete duality in my life so that having two modes of operation was normal for me. I learned this behaviour all those years ago and here I was today, still unconsciously creating it. As a result, I was attracting two wildly different types of people into my life: those who encouraged freedom and expression, and those who sought to control and oppress me. I started to see how I gave all my power away to some people, while being free and fun-loving with others.

Just. Wow.

To help discern whether you may be creating an environment that replicates your past, ask yourself:
- Do I feel oppressed in any area of my life? Romantic partner, friendship, business colleague?
- Do I live in an environment where I'm uncomfortable or partly dissociated?
- Do I feel completely myself with some people, and closed down with others?
- Do I keep secrets from a close loved one or partner?
- Do I censor myself or withhold the truth to avoid punishment?

Diving deeper into this, think about what happens when you're around the people you feel oppressed by:
- What parts of your environment remind you of your abusive past?
- When you feel oppressed, what is that you don't say or do? Is this what you withheld from your abuser as well?

- Does this oppressive environment feel familiar or even comfortable?
- Do you find yourself escaping the oppressive environment? Perhaps you work extra hours, visit friends a lot or take trips away
- Do some people affect your mood more than others? E.g., some may be very uplifting, and you desire to feel that way more often, and others evoke fear, suppression or even apprehension

I found myself manifesting many dishonest and domineering relationships where I gave my power away or felt unsafe because I was replicating learned behaviours and dynamics from the past. Once I realised I was doing this, it instantly became unbearable. I mean, I just worked out I was co-creating my abusive dynamic again! I took action and within the space of a few months, I extracted myself from these oppressive relationships. I promised myself I'd never live a double life again. In that moment, I fused the two realities and healed another layer of my trauma in this incredibly complex and interesting journey.

So, I ask you, are you ready to see your life for what it is? Could you be creating a double life without knowing it?

PART TWO WAVE THREE

I Just Don't Care Anymore. What A Relief

Nobody has a right to infringe on your personal experience. It's not their job to understand you, but it is your job to deeply understand yourself.

I used to be a master at diffusing situations to keep myself safe. I made it my business to manage potentially volatile situations to the best of my ability, and I knew what to say to each of my abusers to alleviate tension and prevent further abuse. The skill saved my life many times in the past, but it was hard to let go. This meant, post-abuse, I spent too much precious time and energy managing and anticipating the emotions of others. Back then, it was for survival. Now it had become exhausting.

When I started to heal, I realised I was still exhibiting this behaviour, and it was having a detrimental effect on me. Realistically, I had no control over what other people thought or did. I was my own person and so were they. If everyone on earth is having their unique and individual experience, what right did I have to infringe on that or try to manage it for them? And why did I need to make it my responsibility?

So, I stopped. I simply stopped trying to manage everyone around me. And you know what? It felt amazing. I reasoned that if anyone was projecting shame, blame or disappointment onto me, and I sincerely didn't deserve it, why did I have to accept it as the truth? The answer is, I didn't. I could simply detach from that narrative and let them have their own experience while I have mine. This is possible for anyone because when we bring conscious awareness to anything, it can only affect us if we allow it to.

I ask you this. Where in your life could you be doing this right now? Are there people in your life who take advantage of you or feed off this anticipation? Something to think about.

The Art Of Leaving People Behind

*One action towards your healing affirms to the Universe that you have faith.
That you know your pain can be healed.*

A little-known truth is that, as you heal, you no longer tolerate the things you once did. As you cultivate discernment and value yourself more, you stop accepting the blame for things you didn't do. And the people close to you? They have to learn to receive you differently. And some of them may not be prepared to do so.

As my self-worth came online, I discovered an innate ability to see through the manipulations and mind games people had been playing with me. I got to a point where I simply wouldn't tolerate certain behaviours anymore, so I stopped participating. At the same time, I found more compassion for myself and for people in general, and experienced a deeper connection and love for humanity. Not only that, I started to feel genuine self-love, something truly miraculous for someone like me. I finally realised I was worth more than what I'd been accepting in my relationships. And I had to face the harsh reality of letting some of them go.

In some of my relationships, my wounded self was all they knew. Once I healed those aspects of myself, certain people found it challenging to be around me. My suffering was a hook they'd attached themselves to. They wanted me incapacitated to some degree and in need of them forever. But I didn't want to stay bound to my suffering and pain. It was stifling and in opposition to my healing. I was forced to end many friendships and relationships because I knew they couldn't accept the healed version of me.

This can be one of the hardest things to do because, to some degree, a co-dependency was formed between these people and our trauma. They were with us during the hard times, and a shoulder to cry on when we were overwhelmed or felt we couldn't do life on our own. They played an important role in our lives and helped us find ourselves and come to this point. The question is, can they evolve and grow with us, too? We must decide who stays in our life and who we need to move away from for our own health and healing.

It's important to understand that not everyone who fits this description is a bad person. If you find it hard to see who has your best interests at heart, here are some questions you may like to reflect on:

- Do you feel deep down that some relationships are not good for you?
- Do you feel like you're not yourself around certain people?

- Are you willing to stay in a toxic, co-dependent relationship because you feel you owe it to them for being there for you?
- Do you stifle your own healing to please others?
- Do you act broken to keep this relationship alive?
- How much stress are you under when they are around?
- What would it mean if you were to completely surrender your pain story and surround yourself with people who support your healing and growth?
- How much of a difference would that make to your life?

I learned a valuable lesson through this stage of my healing. The people we invite into our lives have a huge impact on us, and no one has more influence and impact than a partner. Their attitude towards us will make or break our life, no question about it. It's paramount that we choose a compatible, loving and supportive partner to uplift, inspire and encourage us at every point in our journey. Our life depends on it and the right partner can be a wonderful gift, even if it means letting go of a toxic relationship to receive it. When I removed certain relationships from my life, it was only a matter of weeks before my life felt lighter, easier and more enjoyable. I was no longer weighed down by who I thought I had to be. I could just be me.

Wave 4

Becoming Present and Leaving the Past

*We get so caught up in the right and the wrong
that we miss the blessing in front of us.*

You've faced the reality of your past, begun to detoxify your mind, body and spirit and you're starting to recognise your self-worth. You've achieved so much already, and I hope you're proud of how far you've come.

In Wave 4, we look at the deeper, more complex issues and nuanced behaviours that can arise during deep healing, such as:
- Resistance to release
- What it means to be present
- Co-existing with triggers
- How to live with the remnants of trauma and avoid going backwards
- Subconscious patterns and sabotaging behaviours that emerge when we claim our power back

Don't forget, we're discovering a part of ourselves that has been suppressed for a long time. As we meet who we truly are for the first time, it's normal to grieve the person we're saying goodbye to. We're unravelling deeply ingrained, long-held patterns and behaviours that don't serve us anymore, so we need to be gentle with ourselves.

Are you ready to own your power and master your reality?

It Gets Better, Then Worse, Then Better

Why would we choose to replay a horrible memory over and over again? Because we've attached so much importance to it. On some level, we desire this. If we didn't, it wouldn't play so effortlessly in our minds.

Often, the more progress we make with releasing trauma, the more our subconscious triggers fire up and fight back, which is exasperating. I felt like I was finally making good progress, only to be dragged ten steps backwards again. This push and pull reaction is because our wounded self has been in charge for a long time and doesn't want to let go. But this part of us only ever makes decisions from a place of fear. If we keep placating it, we'll continue succumbing to the fear and be unable to make any decisions or move forward at all.

How I reframed it

I intentionally changed my thoughts around my frustration with taking ten steps backwards. I took a new approach. Whenever I regressed, rather than feel frustrated with myself and judgemental towards my journey, I practised patience and self-compassion instead. I realised that when I regressed, I was *protecting* myself from a particularly traumatic or hidden memory that was painful to release. My subconscious anticipated the gravity of what I was about to see in the form of a flashback, and my wounded self was afraid to confront it. I began to think of it like a metaphorical sky dive. My mind said, *'No way! I'm not jumping out of that plane, and you can't make me!'* Could I really blame that part of myself for holding on? Of course not. Judging wasn't helpful and getting frustrated about it wasn't fair to myself, either. I had to show up with patience, compassion and understanding. I had to be capable enough to transmute and release it.

Current versus past emotions

Many times, the difficult memories that make us want to retreat and protect ourselves are overwhelming because the memory is too painful, we feel too much shame or it's too emotionally intense to recall. The common thread here is *excess*. It's a physical sensation we can feel in our bodies, but it's often not related to our present moment at all. It might not even be how we feel about the experience today. These emotions are a reflection of the intense feelings and reactions we had *during the traumatic event*. It's *how our bodies felt when we first endured the abuse or experienced the trauma*. For example, we think we're angry today at what happened in the past, but that anger was created when we first experienced the trauma.

These trapped emotions and excess energy have been lying dormant since the initial abuse. We're simply observing them for the first time.

Our job now is to embrace our memories with love, feel the feelings that arise and allow them to pass. And they always pass if you let them. After this happened to me a few times, I recognised that regression was actually a gift. It meant I was digging into deeper layers of my trauma, and I was one step closer to fully healing and reclaiming my life in its entirety. Every time I faced a particularly difficult or painful memory, I felt stronger, more capable and more powerful. I gained a level of confidence I didn't have before and found I was no longer being bullied by my memories.

Can you see how reframing our thoughts around a particular setback can completely change the game and move us from a place of frustration to a place of empowerment? A simple shift in our cognitive frame can illuminate the path and encourage acceptance for wherever we are in the healing journey.

Should You Stay Or Should You Grow?

We make choices every moment of the day.
With every thought, action and word,
we're making a choice.

We all reach a wonderful point in our healing journey where we recognise, in real time, that our default patterns and behaviours are trying to emerge. You know, the ones that keep us stuck in the same old loop? It's actually exciting when this happens because it means we have a choice. Do we stick with the old behaviours that we've repeated a million times before? Or do we embrace a new way that allows us to prosper and grow? What do we believe ourselves to be worthy of?

Before we make this decision, let's first acknowledge the monumental achievement this choice symbolises. Because, to make the choice at all, we have to recognise we have free will, which has probably taken a long time and a lot of work to achieve. However, some behaviours could still prevent us from going the whole way.

Defaulting to guilt and shame

As discussed in Wave 3, guilt and shame are some of the most common emotional responses to abuse. It takes time, effort and a considered approach to release them, which is what this healing journey is all about. We eventually reach a level of consciousness where we no longer attach these emotions to our abuse. However, because we're all human, sometimes it's tempting to drop back into them. In these cases, it's less about an authentic emotion related to trauma, and more about an addictive behaviour response.

If we're choosing to respond to situations from a place of shame or guilt, it could be because we're not willing to embrace our own strength. We may not be ready to release the familiar.

Unhealthy attachments

One of the uncomfortable realities of being an abuse victim is we often form a strong attachment to our victim identity. We get used to people perceiving and responding to us in a certain way, and sometimes it's hard to let it go. We might receive extra love, attention and nurturing while we're in a victimised state. It becomes comforting and familiar, and perhaps we even enjoy the attention. But when we're whole and healed, this attention stops. The temptation to fall back into a victimised state of mind is real.

So, what should we do if we feel this temptation? Simply acknowledge an old pattern emerging and gracefully allow it to dissolve. When we step away from being the victim, we give ourselves the opportunity to be so much more. Eventually, we regard ourselves as a whole, healed and healthy individual who is worthy of happiness and love. When we make the switch and choose to no longer be 'that' person, it changes our lives.

Fear of the past

There comes a point where we become so familiar with our own process of healing that we no longer fear what our mind, body or spirit has to share with us. In the early stages of my healing, when my flashbacks were the most severe and intense, I lived in constant dread of what I was going to see next. I was placing myself in a position of powerlessness where I was back to being a victim again, but instead of having an abuser, it was me dispensing the punishment. When I saw this happening, I consciously reduced my fear by *choosing* to switch it off. It was my choice whether I stayed in fear or not. I chose not. Full disclosure, I could only do this after significant work once I'd reached the place of feeling more in control of my healing process.

I trained myself to understand that no matter how challenging or confronting the memory, or how visceral my response was, if I surrendered and allowed it to be released, it would always pass.

PART TWO WAVE FOUR

Avoiding responsibility

As I spoke about earlier in the book, I was an absolute master at avoiding making decisions or connecting with my intuition. I was so scared of being wrong that I constantly looked for someone else to make the choice for me. I outsourced so many of my decisions and it didn't matter who to, a friend, a family member or even a stranger. As long as they were willing to tell me what to do, I was happy to let them!

Even after years of doing the work, this behaviour still emerges from time to time because I had so much brainwashing connected to it. But I was on a mission to fully and completely heal, so I had to learn to make my own decisions and back myself one hundred per cent. And you know what? Once I started doing this, it really wasn't so scary. In fact, I became quite comfortable with making mistakes and accepting responsibility.

If we ever find ourselves avoiding decisions, we need to investigate the reasons why. We can do so much work on ourselves but still carry ingrained toxic behaviours that stop us from stepping into our full power. Today is the day to start making decisions, follow our gut and back ourselves. The action is so small, yet the result is life changing.

And remember, as we discussed in Wave 3, making mistakes is a natural part of life. It's healthy to experience this and learn that we won't be punished for them—an important lesson for any survivor.

Spending all your time in the past

I've heard it said that we're at our most present during early childhood and old age. I believe it's because the beginning and end of our lives are when we're most attuned to our inner world. As we age, we become less preoccupied with external factors and the opinions of others. We're more centred in our own identity. It's as if we shed the layers of societal expectations we accumulate in life, and we can finally just be ourselves.

On the flip side, as children, we often approach life with a carefree attitude and a willingness to take risks. We're driven by our emotions rather than rational thoughts, and we approach new experiences with a sense of wonder and excitement! Children are unencumbered by responsibilities, constraints and preconceived notions. We're curious about everything and we interact with the world around us in a more playful and uninhibited way, our minds constantly expanding as we learn new things. This period of childhood is full of possibility, potential, discovery and adventure.

So, what happens when we're exposed to a predator during these formative years? Well, for the lucky ones, we remember, we do the work and we heal. For others, we suppress, and we block. Perhaps we pretend it never happened at all. And we live symptomatically for the remaining years of our life—a sad existence.

When abuse takes place as a child or a teenager, we sometimes don't comprehend the full gravity of it until we're in our twenties or thirties, or even much older. When our trauma surfaces as an adult, our focus and attention are drawn away from our present reality into the past. We spend more time reliving moments we spent as a child and teenager than we do in our current reality as an adult. Why is this important? Because there has to be a point where we stop paying our attention to our traumatised younger years.

There's a fine balance between respecting the time needed to heal and reclaiming control over our lives. Ultimately, the less time we spend dwelling on past struggles, the better, but only after we've put in the work to process and overcome them. The faster we can accept and embrace our current circumstances, and the precious gift of the present, the more fulfilling our lives can be. By focusing on the present moment and fully engaging with our lives now, we open ourselves up to the endless possibilities that exist around us.

Verbalising your suffering and story

The words we speak aloud carry immense power. They affirm our thoughts and shape our reality by bringing our manifestations to life. So, if we're constantly talking about our past and our pain, what kind of message are we sending out into the world? And what, in turn, do we magnetise toward ourselves? At what point do we stop bringing the energy of our abusive past into our present and future?

I'll never forget the moment that, while sitting in meditation one day, a thought announced itself loudly in my mind.

"Stop talking about it!"

I was so startled my eyes popped right open and my breath caught in my chest. Was I just being scolded by my own mind?

The answer was yes!

I started to reflect on just how much I talked about my past and, no surprises here, it was much more than I realised. I should have been focusing on creating new memories in my present reality, but talking about my past was such a hard habit to break.

So, I stopped.
Right then and there, I stopped talking about it as much.

It's worth mentioning that in the early stages of healing, particularly Waves 1 to 3, it's important to talk about aspects of your trauma so you receive the right support. There is a point, however, when this no longer serves us and we're just dragging our past into our present.

That day, I reached that point.
So, I stopped. And I was much better for it.

Co-Existing With Triggers And Flashbacks

Trauma manifests in our lives regardless of whether we do the work or not. If we do the work, we quite literally have our trauma in the palm of our hand. If we don't, however, the trauma decides—and we have doubled the amount of trauma we experience in one lifetime.

I believe two clearly defined aspects of my being exist inside me; the traumatised girl who carries the memories and emotions of every terrible thing that happened to her, and the healthy, healed, empowered and evolved woman who exists in the present day. The traumatised girl acts as a brave informant and she wants me to understand what happened, why it happened and how it's holding me back.

She encourages me to find compassion and forgiveness, recognise the false beliefs that have plagued me and, most importantly, live an enjoyable life. Anything that stands in the way of that, she's going to let me know about.

I promised myself I would never ignore or dismiss the traumatised girl. I vowed to remain open to whatever she needed to show me, no matter how confronting, and I agreed to transmute all pain and suffering through my body so it's gone forever. I no longer wanted to carry the heavy burdens of the past. By relentlessly showing up for myself, I built a loving, trusting relationship with this aspect of myself, and I allow her to show me anything that needs to be released. This has not been easy, and I've shed layers of myself over and over again. And each time I do, I come closer to the truth of who I really am. By having a relationship with my inner traumatised girl, I have opened myself up to understanding and learning more, and giving myself permission to heal.

When we build and nurture this relationship with ourselves, we claim our sovereignty. And it's not a one-off occurrence. It's a way of life. We're choosing to connect with and acknowledge our past without being ashamed of it. This alone gives us great strength. Making this promise can feel like signing up for never-ending work, but it only feels like this because we've been holding onto so much for so long.

What I can tell you is this: No matter how dark and traumatic your abuse, in time, the memory does fade.

Here's an example of how, even after so much healing work has been done, we can still be triggered, but it doesn't have to consume us like it once did. While visiting a park one day, I passed a side passageway of an abandoned-looking building. I was almost past it when I caught a glimpse of a tall staircase leading to an emergency door. The sight of it sent shivers down my spine. In a matter of seconds, my body was flooded with adrenaline. Part of me wanted to shake it off and ignore it, but I knew from working through my healing process that my traumatised self was trying to communicate something to me involving this stairwell. I knew not to ignore these signals. Did I become frustrated because I thought this part of my journey and healing should be over? No. Because I understand this is a lifelong journey. Did I fear my reaction? No. Because fear is a choice. Did I seek to talk about it? No, because I'd already talked at length, and I recognised that continuously talking about my trauma story can be addictive and unhelpful. Instead, I calmly took control of my mind and body, took a moment to feel everything going on within me and sat with 'why' I felt stressed by the emergency exit. In return, I was given information about my past and the trapped trauma that needed to be released. My body was relaying the message about a similar stairwell I was taken to by the abusers, but it took conscious awareness for me to receive it.

I believe we all have an inner wisdom that brings forward the information we need exactly when we need it. If we choose to ignore it or put our head in the sand, it keeps circling around in our minds and manifesting as stress in our bodies. Over many years, unprocessed trauma can result in a whole host of behavioural side effects, substance dependencies and physical and mental illnesses.

If we want to completely transmute our suffering and find liberation, we need to be prepared to bring conscious awareness to our triggers when they show up and let go of any attachment we may have to a timeline. Healing is not an end goal. It's a continuous journey.

PART TWO WAVE FOUR

Regression And Environmental Triggers

How much of our past reality do we perpetuate via our words? Is the desire to share so compulsive that we must constantly speak our past into the future? Sometimes, deep contemplation and silence are all that is needed.

Let's talk about regressions. They do happen, and it's nothing to be alarmed about. In fact, it's a normal part of the healing process when dealing with extreme trauma. Regressions can happen months, even years, after a healing crisis. The important thing is to not panic about it and to know deep down that you're going to be just fine. In case you're wondering what I mean by regressions, I'm referring to stepping back into your healing journey, to the point you feel you never left it.

It's normal to hope that, once we've done the hard work, we can be free of flashbacks for good. It's not always the case, but they definitely do reduce. One of my main triggers causing me to regress was the amount of time I spent processing the environment around me. If I saw anything that reminded me of my past, my heart started pounding like a jackhammer and I'd be re-traumatised all over again.

This looked like:
- Feeling constantly unsafe, even around loving and protective men
- Being worried someone was going to hurt me in my sleep

- Being suspicious of anyone who vaguely resembled my abuser
- Keeping a low profile and remaining anonymous wherever possible
- Linking unrelated experiences together to form paranoid views
- Panicking at loud noises

I didn't want to accept I'd be on high alert for the rest of my life, anticipating the next trigger that would set me off. The constant hypervigilance was exhausting. I knew I was projecting my fears onto situations where it wasn't warranted.

I asked myself, *at what point does this stop?*

Could I choose to be present in the moment, rather than reliving the past?
Could I accept I was ok, safe and protected? And not being led into violence?
Could I ask for help from others or my loving partner?

I noticed that every time my thoughts turned, I became quiet, withdrawn and absent. I was dissociating. I also recognised that this behaviour encouraged and enabled the victimised part of myself.

What helped me was:
- Communicating with my partner, a close friend or a family member every time something triggered me. I explained I would be identifying certain behaviours in that moment to become more present
- Paying close attention to how my body felt and how it changed in these moments

- Concentrating on my breathing and moving from short, shallow breaths to long, slow, deep breaths
- Shifting my focus to something beautiful nearby: a pretty flower or a beautiful tree. I would smile to myself as if to say, *'it's ok, I love you, and we are in control of the situation now.'* I affirmed that the wise, responsible, adult part of me was stepping up to help the wounded teenage girl navigate through the fear
- If centred enough, I closed my eyes or went into my thoughts, took a deep breath and asked myself, *'what is triggering me at this moment and what information do you have to help me at this moment?'* I knew I was being triggered for a reason and this helped me extract why

Focusing on being fully embodied meant I couldn't be led astray or convinced to do anything I didn't want to do. It gave me the power to bring myself back to the present, switch my narrative and see my environment the way I wanted to, from a place of safety and protection.

We all have the ability to create a reality that is safe and allows us to flourish. It's time to take back control of our minds.

METAMORPHOSIS

Did You Just Reprogram Yourself?

I have rebuilt myself with nothing but love.

How often are we unconsciously recreating abuse dynamics in our lives?

I was almost eighteen months into my healing journey when I realised I was *still* creating traumatic environments for myself and being plagued by the same old issues I'd worked so hard to release. Ouch!

This looked like:
- Waking up from nightmares, disoriented and gasping for air
- An inability to relax in my surroundings, and paranoia while I was out in the world
- Paranoid thoughts and deep suspicion of the people in my life
- Imagining horrible scenarios where my abusers found me and took me back
- Gruesome images flashing in my mind for a split second then disappearing
- Intense emotional outbursts of fear, grief and pain—all coming out at once
- I'd expected these symptoms to decrease as I healed, but they hadn't at all. Why was I still being haunted by them after all this work I'd done? What was I missing?

I began to ask different questions:
- Have I retained brainwashing programs that encourage me to perpetuate these cycles and keep me orientated towards negative and disempowering experiences?
- Could I be reprogramming myself constantly?
- Could there be internal blocks stopping me from accepting and experiencing peace?
- Can I really allow myself to be healed and happy?

When the answer came to me, it was illuminating. I was playing out the abuse dynamic with situations that were familiar to me, and it was exactly what my abusers wanted me to do.

I started to see the patterns and themes that were recurring in my life on a daily basis:
- Constriction and control
- Lack of connection
- Secrecy and confusion
- Objectification and overt sexualisation
- Service to others in the form of giving energy away
- Constantly explaining my actions
- Seeking permission to act or do certain things that were important to me

I'd replicated what I lived through with my abusers all those years ago and brought it into my home. Again. Not only had I created an environment that *felt* similar, but I was unconsciously simulating situations I'd been abused in. It's no wonder my nightmares and flashbacks hadn't subsided. I had the sudden urge to remove myself and escape like I did all those years ago.

How to regain control

It sounds like a simple solution, but I found journalling incredibly helpful, particularly in revealing who in my life was contributing to this dynamic. It also helped me to not gaslight myself because I could refer to my journals and see a physical record of my thoughts and emotions about a situation at any time. It became a safe space for self-expression where I could see certain truths I had previously denied.

Here's an exercise I used to help examine my environment. I thought about when in my daily life I felt blamed, objectified, confused, suppressed or controlled, then asked myself:

- Who am I with?
- What are they saying to make me feel this way?
- Do they have a close relationship with me?
- Can I safely distance myself from them or remove myself from the situation?

I also thought about everyday scenarios and how my body—not my mind—responded to them? For example, when I walk in my front door, when I go to sleep at night, when I'm relaxing or doing something on my own, does my energy shift? Do I act any differently? Am I on edge, hyper-aware or self-conscious? What actions am I taking?

I then thought back to my abusers and asked myself:

- How did they speak to me and what did they say to me?
- What feelings did I have in my body at the time?
- Did my energy shift when I saw them?
- What kind of experiences did I have with them?

There were always similarities.

While this exercise is confronting, if we do it honestly, it can help us change patterns and set us back on our true path. When I fully committed to journalling and reflecting in this way, some of my biggest shifts in perception occurred and I could see so clearly the toxic cycle I was stuck in. And when I say big shifts, I mean huge. I left the partner I was with, dissolved toxic friendships, moved house, sold my car and even threw out half my wardrobe! It was the wake-up call and reset I needed. It set me on a path toward a completely new life, which was radically different to the one before. This exercise stopped me from recreating my programmed past and allowed me to create a new reality for myself that was filled with new experiences, kind people, self-care, love and respect. Plus, my flashbacks and neurosis dropped considerably.

In addition to journalling, I developed a number of deep spiritual practices to ground and guide me towards what I wanted to embody.

Love.
Acceptance.
Self-care.
Self-respect.

I found I could go without these practices for a certain period of time—which will be different for everyone—but if I stopped for long periods, I felt disconnected and disembodied. I needed their support and structure and when I didn't have them, the wounded patterns emerged, and my trauma seeped back in and filled the cracks my spiritual practices had left.

If you've been doing the work to heal your trauma but suspect you may be slipping into avoidance or unhealthy coping mechanisms, here are some common indicators:
- You feel agitated and hardened. People irritate you and you believe everything is their fault
- You want to be alone all the time, feeling the need to be away from people
- You start having flashbacks
- You feel the urge to speak about your past, even after all the work you've done
- You're depressed, deflated and unmotivated

If you notice any of these emerging, consider them a warning that you need to take time out and briefly connect with your past again. I guarantee something is there that requires releasing. I recommend doing this check-in with yourself on a regular basis to pre-empt any avoidance behaviours that could become a problem later. What may seem like a tiny ember can turn into a blazing inferno pretty quickly, so you need to watch closely and be ready to control the situation if need be.

The good thing is, releasing this resurfaced trauma doesn't mean going back to square one. It just requires a refocus. Eventually, you come to the point where you can see just how profoundly your life has changed and you feel like you've been given a second chance, an opportunity to experience a whole new life within the same lifetime.

Hard to believe, isn't it? But based on my experience, it's entirely true. We can release the dissociating, the heavy emotions and the old behaviour patterns that we were once so attached to. We can become so healed that the trauma fades from our memory like ink from the pages of a well-worn book.

Although I still have aspects of my trauma emerge for release, for the most part I enjoy peace, contentment, liberation and love. Now that is one incredible reward.

Beware Of Spiritual Bypassing

Authentically broadening our consciousness and genuinely improving our thinking is the ultimate anecdote to trauma.

I believe spiritual and self-healing practices are helpful for anyone, but particularly for those who are working through deep trauma. Having said that, it can be tempting to attach ourselves so strongly to these practices that we believe we've surpassed anything negative, and we no longer have to acknowledge the bad things that happen in our lives. This way of thinking can become problematic and lead to a lack of authenticity and self-awareness. It's often described as spiritual bypassing.

If we find ourselves spiritually bypassing, we're escaping from reality or suppressing anything we don't want to feel, rather than addressing the emotions and working through them directly. This can look like:
- Denying or minimising our negative emotions and focusing only on positive or uplifting experiences. E.g., Suppressing anger or sadness rather than releasing those emotions
- Over-identifying with a spiritual persona and using it to define our identity, to the point of ignoring

other aspects. For example, becoming so attached to a particular spiritual tradition or belief system that it becomes the sole focus of our lives, to the detriment of other relationships or personal growth
- Disconnecting from the world around us to maintain a sense of purity or detachment

So, while having spiritual and self-healing practices are important tools for growth and healing, just be conscious of the temptation to attach so strongly that you end up suppressing your authentic feelings. If you find yourself forming too strong an attachment to this, go back to some of the earlier concepts in this book to lovingly connect with whatever is arising and release it. Remember, you are a strong, healthy, healed individual. You have the power to release anything from your past with intention and respect.

The Unspoken Vows We All Made

Everything that comes to us in life is an offer.
Even our suffering.
It's up to us whether we accept it.

It wasn't until late in my healing journey that I unpacked my own vows, beliefs and promises and saw I was still wearing the unconscious protective armour I'd acquired from my past experiences. I wasn't serving myself in the present day.

I began to recognise I was still holding strong beliefs such as:
- I never want a family because they'll end up being hurt
- I hate men and women and I don't trust them
- I never want to be played again
- When I trust someone, they hurt me deeply
- I will never share my feelings because I get hurt

Are there any statements here you identify with or perhaps feel triggered by? After so much healing work, do these small statements still feel larger than life? These beliefs and programs can be some of the last to be surrendered because they plant their roots deep in our subconscious and spread out like a weed. You can imagine the negative impact they have on future potential relationships.

So, how do you release them? I encourage you to sit and deeply feel into the protective armour you constructed at the time of the abuse. You created it to protect yourself, but now it needs to be dissected and dismantled. You could have created ten, a hundred or even a thousand protective belief statements which have been materialising through dysfunctional behaviours and dishonest connections in your present day.

One of the most effective ways to rescind any vows or oaths you subconsciously made is to speak the words out loud. When directed with intention, the words you speak can change your life.

Here are some powerful statements to help dissolve existing belief statements.

I renounce, revoke and recall any vows, promises and contracts that are no longer in alignment with my highest good.

I now revoke, renounce, recall any vows, promises and contracts that keep me from connecting to my highest purpose and full expression, and so it is.

These overarching prayers and statements neutralise and rescind unconscious patterns, beliefs and behaviours. I encourage you to write your own and repeat them out loud often.

We All Have A Choice

Choice starts with thought.

After such a deeply profound healing journey, we realise that the final thing we're given is a choice. Do we leave the past in the past, surrender all the fears and attachments and choose our new reality? Or do we persist in dragging our baggage into this new life we're creating?

Here's an example of what I mean. When I believed the past was still haunting me, I automatically attributed my nightmares, poor sleep and paranoia to my trauma, meaning part of me was still fearing the past and what may surface next. By allowing those wounded aspects to retain an element of control over me, I never felt *completely* in control. These are the kinds of disempowering and victimised thought patterns we work so hard to release.

I had done my work.
I wanted a way to end the cycle once and for all.

For two years, my life pretty much revolved around purging my trauma, going through releases, working out what happened to me and slowly stitching my memories together like a patchwork quilt. All this investigative work instilled strong behavioural patterns that were helpful at the time but were now becoming a problem. I couldn't have them overshadowing my current reality. I had to let go of them so I could find the peace I was looking for.

Then, one day it dawned on me:
- *What if I had actually healed and become whole?*
- *What if what I was searching for was already here and the peace and harmony I'd been seeking had arrived?*
- *What if my actual reality was fine, but I kept trying to create a different one with my traumatic past?*

Something to think about.

Integrating Your Shadow With Your Light

Darkness gives context to the light. Our appreciation of peace and harmony within our lives can only be drawn from the existence of the opposite.

Before we move into Wave 5, I want to talk about integrating, accepting and loving all parts of us, even if we still want to deny one part of us. Are we happy to own ninety per cent of ourselves, but willing to disconnect from and disown the other ten per cent because we believe it will always be broken and wounded? And do we still consider that shadow side to be a part of us?

A Healer once asked me if I loved all the light within me. I asked her what she meant by light. She explained it as the qualities generally considered as positive and good, like being kind, caring and patient. I responded, 'Of course!' It felt easy and effortless to tune into and accept those parts of myself. She then asked me if I loved all the darkness within me, the qualities I may not be so quick to accept about myself, such as insecurity, self-doubt, shame, having a lack of boundaries and so on. I considered it for a moment before reluctantly giving her my answer. 'No, I don't.' My response surprised me. I mean, after all my work, I thought I'd developed compassionate, unconditional love for myself, but here I was denying and rejecting a natural part of my personality. I asked myself *why don't I love all of me?* The answer began to surface. I held a belief that only some of my shadow was mine.

This is where things got interesting.

Deep in my subconscious, I had compartmentalised aspects of my personality and shadow self that I didn't want to claim as part of me. I was still carrying them, and they were still being expressed through me. However, I was avoiding taking responsibility for them. I was in denial, plain and simple. Aspects of my personality were forged in the fire of my abuse, and I was pretending they didn't exist.

Talk about an a-ha moment! Hot on the heels of that realisation was another big one:

If I never claimed that part of myself, I could always hold it at a distance. And it would always remain out of my control.

Think about this for a moment.

Your subconscious mind says, *my lack of boundaries has nothing to do with me, because I was programmed to have none.* But your conscious mind says, *I hate that I have no boundaries.* Who is responsible here? Who is going to heal and integrate this part of yourself? Is it you? Or should you leave it to the people who abused you?

You already know the answer.

Only we can rescue ourselves and integrate our shadows with our light. The only real option here is to radically and unashamedly accept all parts of us, no matter how they got there. We developed these shadows because of our trauma and now we need to take the leap of faith, put aside the anger and embrace it all.

So now I ask you, which shadow aspects do you accept as a natural part of you and which ones are you blaming your abusers for? Where might you be disowning your shadow and, as a result, giving power to the past?

Here is an example of a journal entry I made when doing shadow discovery work.

Question: I believe that without any abuse, my natural shadow aspects would be:
- *I'm short-tempered*
- *I don't listen to people or I tune out and lose interest quickly*

- *I'm loud and overly confident*
- *I like to be the centre of attention*

Question: Because of the abuse, I believe I developed these shadow aspects:
- *I give too much of myself to others, expecting to receive little in return*
- *I lack boundaries and allow people to take advantage of me*
- *I internalise my anger and find it difficult to speak my truth because I fear lashing out*
- *I go through life in fear*
- *I descend into self-pity easily*

This exercise helps you peel back the layers of your shadow side to discover which aspects you take ownership of as yours and which you don't. As survivors of abuse, it's so important to accept and embrace all that we are, regardless of the injustice or anger we may feel, or how many powerful stories we've attached to our abuse.

During my healing, I had to accept many parts of myself I didn't particularly like. I accepted responsibility for things I was coerced to do. These shadow aspects were not technically mine, but I accepted them and took responsibility for them, anyway.

Yes, I accept this shadow side of my personality.
Yes, I did do that, and I accept that I did.
And so on and so forth.

Today, every aspect of me shows up. Despite the injustice, the abuse, the words and deeds of the past, I lovingly and wholeheartedly accept the person I am.

Wave 5

Claiming Your Life Back

*Deep pain and suffering have an expiry date,
and we've reached ours.*

Here we are. The fifth and final wave. This is where we transcend from the groundwork of healing to taking full responsibility for our lives every day from here on out. This wave is about life post-healing, and how to transition from being in the trenches of trauma to a maintenance plan that sets us up to thrive. We learn how to support and embrace the new, healthier version of ourselves while honouring our journey and everything we've been through so far.

It's time to well and truly let go of those stubborn, negative belief patterns that tell us we're unable to heal, that we're too weak or powerless in this world or that the work we've done still isn't enough. These thoughts lead to one place only, and that is *nowhere*.

So, what do we do?
We take back control.

We've done the work.

We've purged our trauma, and we've healed from all sorts of atrocities.

It's now our time.
We're laying our inner victim to rest.
We no longer acquiesce to a story of suffering or victimisation.

We feel safe, happy, at peace.

Every single person on this planet is creating their reality every day, through their thoughts, beliefs, words and actions. We can, at any moment, define a new world for ourselves and consciously choose to leave the past behind. It really is that simple.

The only thing getting in the way of it is *us*.

In Wave 5, we uncover:
- The importance of our thoughts, words and actions
- How we can cast a new reality for ourselves
- Applying radical self-acceptance and love
- What becomes of life from here

Would you like a life where you feel so joyful, people question whether anything terrible happened to you at all? Getting to this stage is possible, and the only person who can make the final leap is you.

Will you take it?
Are you ready to leave the past and step into your full power?
Are you ready to take complete responsibility in your life?

PART TWO WAVE FIVE

Are you ready to create a new and abundant reality?

It's time.
Take my hand, we're almost there.
We're almost home.

Control Your Present, Create Your Future

If every second of every day we are presented an opportunity to think and feel different, then by calculation we have 86,400 opportunities a day.

I want to share an interesting concept with you around time, and it starts with a simple question. Do you believe we have any control over our future? Most of us would probably say no. We may even feel challenged by this answer because the future has always been overshadowed by a traumatic past.

But here's what we don't factor in.
The past is being created right now.
In this present moment.

Each of today's thoughts, decisions, words and actions are creating the past we'll look back on tomorrow.

This means we no longer have to be passive recipients of circumstance. We can actively make the choices and decisions that positively shape our lives. Once we accept and embrace this power and recognise we can release what no longer serves us, the possibilities for life become endless. Our past no longer has to be defined by abuse. It can be fully defined by us and the choices we make today. Rather than thinking about the future as just good or bad luck, we can put our thoughts and actions into creating a life we desire.

Let's practise this for a moment.

I want you to stop what you're doing, close your eyes and think about the unlimited number of choices available to you right now.

- How do you feel right now? Are you comfortable? Too hot, too cold? Can you change position, grab a blanket or remove a layer of clothing?
- Where are you right now? Can you stand up and move to the left or right? Can you walk away? Can you go somewhere else?
- Who is around you? Can you move further away from them if you don't like them?
- What are you doing? Can you choose a different activity and do that instead?
- What are you eating and drinking? Can you stop consuming those foods and eat something else?
- What are you thinking about? Can you switch your focus?

Can you see how, at any given moment, we're presented with unlimited possibilities? Some people may find this a challenge, particularly those of us who have never been encouraged to be independent, let alone believe we are powerful and have agency over our lives. Entire social structures are built around the idea that we are powerless, and we must suffer and struggle through life. But that's not the truth, is it? We've always had the power. We just didn't know how to claim it. Until now.

So, I ask you.

Will you float through each day unconsciously, letting external influences dictate your life and blow you around like a feather in the breeze? Or will you stop, take an audit of your situation, and intentionally create a past you're proud of? Understanding this concept removes the anxiousness around what happens in the future and brings us back to a point of power, which is now.

Applying Radical Self-Acceptance

It's ludicrous to think I am fighting a battle not with those that hurt me, but with myself.

We've purged so much of the past from our bodies. We've put in the work to recognise our value and feel genuine love toward ourselves, perhaps for the first time ever. What comes next?

It's time to *radically* accept ourselves.
And when I say radical, I really do mean it. Our post-abuse happiness depends on it.
Allow me to share an example.

METAMORPHOSIS

During my years of abuse, my worth was defined entirely by how much of myself I gave my abusers and what I did for them. My body was a commodity and my survival depended on my ability to execute their orders and please them however they saw fit. If I didn't, the consequences were drastic—as you might imagine. The result was I didn't naturally develop a sense of identity or any confidence in who I was as a person. I genuinely believed the only way to be seen, appreciated or validated by anyone was to present myself in a certain way or provide something that directly benefited them. This attachment to the external, to how I looked and what I could do, became a significant part of my self-image and kept me enslaved for a decade post-abuse. I constantly gave to others and received so little in return because I couldn't accept I was enough. This wounded behaviour was one of the hardest to give up.

That is until ...
I learned to apply *radical self-acceptance*.

After years of wrestling with it, I simply decided I was going to accept myself for who I was, no matter what. Every little part of me, even the 'yucky' parts I didn't like.

I accepted I was giving too much.
I accepted all my unappealing behaviours, things I felt ashamed of.
I threw out my list of perfect ways to act in order to be seen as worthy.
I surrendered and accepted the lot.
Instead of judging myself, I laid down my sword and walked away.
And the noise in my head stopped.
Just like that.

Every judgemental thought that had droned on in the background of my brain for years just stopped. And it was incredibly, blissfully silent. The shift was so drastic, I remember the exact moment it happened because I let out a sigh of relief and giggled to myself. *I actually giggled!* But here's the important thing. When I stopped judging myself, and the thoughts stopped churning erratically in my brain, I found I no longer cared for the judgments of others. I experienced a huge shift towards self-acceptance, a complete surrendering to stillness, peace and contentment in being exactly who I was. I stepped into my power at that moment. I became self-governing, self-regulating and most of all self-accepting. I stopped being scared or ashamed of who I was, and I stopped battling with myself. The shame was gone, the guilt was gone, the expectations were gone. It all just left, and I became free.

Often when we embark on a healing journey, we become caught up in chasing a better version of ourselves. Entire industries are built around the idea we should always be dissatisfied with aspects of ourselves, whether it's our finances, our appearance, our relationships or our everyday lives. This works for some people, but not everyone. And when we're dealing with deep trauma, it can be damaging to constantly ride the merry-go-round of 'self-development' because it creates a sense of dissatisfaction with our current state. That's why it's so important to approach the pursuit of healing in a healthy and balanced way. This means being patient as we work towards our goals. Remember, we're striving for progress, not perfection, and we need to honour where we are. For me, no longer judging myself was one of the greatest gifts I could give myself. I had complexities from my past, but that was perfectly ok.

The Importance Of A High Vibration

We all inherently know what keeps our vibration and spirits high. It's the thoughts and decisions we make to avoid this that should be truly examined.

We've all heard the concept that whatever you give out, you ultimately get back. The Law of Attraction expresses this beautifully and succinctly: Like Attracts Like.

Increasing our vibration is one of the most effective ways to attract positive experiences and people into our lives—provided it's done authentically and not through spiritual bypassing. But it also brings rise to what is not at resonance in our lives.

This is where we must be extra mindful of our lifestyle choices, whether it's what we choose to consume, the attitude we adopt or who we spend time with. Our daily habits have a huge impact on our wellbeing and overall vibrational energy. By consciously choosing healthy and positive thoughts, habits, environments and influences, we can avoid perpetuating lower frequencies and shift towards a higher state of being. When we raise our vibration authentically, through kindness and compassion or taking care of ourselves or someone else, it feels genuinely good at a soul level. In time, this high vibrational state resonates much more comfortably, and a lower vibrational state is no longer a match. Things we may have accepted in the past start to disappear from our lives and we don't attract toxic dynamics anymore. In many regards, this can feel like a death, or that people have abandoned us, but what is more likely is we have abandoned the lower vibrational forces that kept us in our trauma and wounding, thus attracting other traumatised people into our lives.

Any old belief patterns or unhealed aspects of our trauma rise and release when we increase our vibration. It requires us to be brave and leave it all behind. Whilst we can seek out healers and energy workers to support us in this work, *we* are the ones who must take responsibility for keeping our vibration high.

Mourning The Old You

True comfort, I mean the peace and harmony you search for, comes not from successfully coping with the degree of trauma you have within your body, but from reaching a place of complete wholeness within, healed of past wounds. That is the only kind of comfort we should ever seek.

As we're alchemizing our trauma and reconnecting with our true selves, it's important to acknowledge what a monumental journey this has been. We're not just closing a chapter on our past, we're finishing an entire book! It's exhilarating and terrifying in equal measure, and it's normal to have no idea what comes next.

To welcome in the new, authentic and empowered version of ourselves, we have to surrender the old. There's no other way to do it. It's normal to feel reluctant about this, but eventually, you come to realise the new, healed version of yourself is the real you. It was always there, just buried beneath layers of trauma and programming. Now you've created a safe space for this part of you to emerge and take flight. And while it's exciting to leave the old behind, it's also normal to want to mourn the old you.

This happened to me multiple times. You see, I knew exactly what it felt like to be the traumatised version of myself. I'd been living that way for years, so it was a comfortable place to be. I knew how to relate to others, how to have relationships and how to navigate life as a traumatised person. I was riddled with insecurities, and I felt lonely and disconnected a lot of the time, but it was still a familiar place to me.

But once I'd healed? The difference was extraordinary. I'd evolved so much from what I used to be that I often didn't recognise myself. It was like discovering the world for the first time. I experimented with upholding boundaries by saying things I'd never said before, such as the word 'No'. I learned to trust myself and honour my needs without feeling selfish about it.

Not only did I have to accept the new me, but the people around me had to accept me too. The new me possessed self-love, self-awareness and even, dare I say it, confidence! And let me tell you, not everyone in my life was comfortable with that. I had to let many relationships and friendships go because they couldn't be supportive of this healthier side of me. And do you know why I was okay with that? Because I knew that my healing was worth more than keeping myself small and manageable for them. Slowly but surely, I became so aligned with this stronger and healthier way of being that I knew I wasn't going to turn back. So, anyone in my life at that time had a choice. They could either come with me and support me, or they got left behind.

And here's where it gets interesting ... It wasn't just my attitude and demeanour that changed. It was also my physical body, and the changes were nothing short of astounding. After two years of purging toxic memories and emotional baggage, I lost weight, my eyes became brighter, and my hair got thicker. And weirdly, my height increased and overall figure drastically changed too! I know that's hard to believe, but that's what happened. Some friends, and even family members, didn't recognise me. My inner work was reflected in my physical body and this was when I knew I was becoming the real me.

I was astonished by how trauma can affect the appearance of our physical bodies, but more so when it's released, how the body responds so positively by restoring us back to balance. This taught me about the true intelligence of the human body and how it always supports you to heal, no matter how damaging and systemic the trauma was. Most importantly, I didn't have to think about any of it. My body just knew what to do.

Throughout this time, significant shifts in my thoughts and inner dialogue also took place. It all became much more gentle, forgiving, and compassionate. Instead of dwelling on my mistakes or perceived shortcomings, I approached myself with kindness and understanding. I found myself thinking:
- It's perfectly fine for me to spend an afternoon sitting on the beach in silence
- I don't really care what people think of me right now
- That person's reaction doesn't bother me
- I don't feel like doing that, so I'm not going to
- I don't want to socialise with people and I'm going to honour these feelings
- I don't think that is a good idea, so I won't do it
- I love my own company

For the first time in my life, I embodied 'self-love'.

I felt different, I looked different, I even spoke differently, but it all felt so natural. It all felt like me. I had found my way home, and I was never going to leave again.

You Are Not Lucky To Be Healed. You Are Worthy

When you realise that control of your life exists solely within your mind, everything becomes an opportunity to embrace more love, more life and more happiness.

'I feel so lucky to have this.'

Have you ever felt that way, or perhaps spoken it out loud? I have. Following my healing crisis, things I never thought possible were happening, and every day felt like a gift. I felt in total alignment with life, and I often caught myself thinking, *I just feel so lucky.*

Let's ponder this for a moment.

The term lucky refers to an outcome or circumstance that occurs purely by chance. It's a fluke of the universe or a stroke of good fortune, nothing to do with effort or merit on the part of the individual. Did I really believe all the work I'd done could be categorised as luck? Absolutely not. I worked for every bit of abundance, freedom and prosperity now coming my way. And when I say, 'I worked for it', I mean, I faced my trauma, disintegrated my wounded patterns, released the beliefs keeping me trapped and suppressed in life and I claimed my full power.

I could not attribute my life to being lucky. My life had turned around because I finally accepted a truth that I'd been groomed to deny for years. I was worthy.

What Becomes Of Life?

Turn your wounds into wisdom.

Every single act of abuse I endured is written in history and frozen in time. Every time something horrible was done to me, it either created a new wound, or reopened an existing scar that later needed to be healed. Some of these wounds were small, others were enormous, but each one deepened a hole I eventually had to dig my way out of. Why am I sharing this? Because if it's true that with every act of violence we become more broken and traumatised, then could it also be true that with every act of healing and love, we're mending and becoming more whole? Could it really be true one way and not the other?

Every action we take toward healing builds on the one before it. Even the simplest acts of love and kindness towards ourselves make a difference.

METAMORPHOSIS

The seeds we plant now bear fruit for years to come, so I implore you to keep showing up for yourself and acknowledging the hard work you've done.

When we reach the point where our past is no longer consuming us, new goals, desires and aspirations take shape. We think about life in a brand-new way and the dreams we never dared to dream step out of the shadows and into the light. Perhaps it's a new job, new hobbies or interests, travel and adventure, maybe even a loving romantic partner? Each of these goals are more authentically aligned to who we are now. We have the opportunity to reframe our abuse any way we want to, and we get a chance, right now, to start our lives anew.

In the same way that my abuse became more extreme as time went on, my healing also became more incredible, powerful and life-enhancing as time went on. Every day, week and month bought new surprises, opportunities and relationships aligned with who I was, not who I was groomed to be. I was blown away by how effortlessly things lined up in my life and how simple it was for me to tap into what felt truthful to me. Every day I created, and still create, the reality of my dreams. If I can overcome my adversity and completely master my life, then so can you.

You don't have to have experienced my trauma to take this lesson. You can have it no matter where you are in life. Always remember that you can not only heal and be whole again, you can also make the decision to dominate life and choose any existence you desire. You are in full control of your world, and you never have to be defined by your past again.

Every single one of us has the option, and the power, to rewrite the wrongs and create an entirely new reality. Life may have given us bad experiences, but we've proven that we can transmute, resurrect and rebuild. Sometimes the most beautiful things in this life are forged from the ashes of what came before. I have taken that approach and applied it to my own life, where I have inverted all their depraved desires. Instead of directing my thoughts and energy into evil and destruction, I channelled mine into creation and love. I flipped the narrative, made the impossible, possible and created the most incredible life for myself.

They directed their power to the dark.
I applied mine to the light.

Forgiveness Prayer

*If I seek to hear 'I'm sorry' from those who hurt me,
I am simultaneously harbouring injustice, resentment
and anger whilst waiting.
In order to be happy, I need to release myself,
not 'wait' to be released.*

It's said that carrying resentment is like drinking poison and waiting for the other person to die. And while it's a recognisable truth, I'm the first to admit it's not always easy, and finding release is absolutely crucial. I created a mantra, almost like a forgiveness prayer, that I use to release resentment, reroute my neural pathways and physically change the energy charge within my body. I ask myself these questions and I answer yes to every single one, whether I feel that way or not. I use it to affirm forgiveness and encourage my mind, body and spirit to be free.

METAMORPHOSIS

*Do I forgive all those that hurt me, intentionally
or unintentionally, through thought, word
or deed?*
Yes.

*Do I forgive myself for all things, knowingly or
unknowingly, through thought, word or deed?*
Yes.

*Do I forgive myself for the abuse that happened
to me?*
Yes.

*Do I forgive myself for who I am today as a
result of my abuse?*
Yes.

*Do I forgive everyone who allowed me to
enter my abusive situation, knowingly or
unknowingly?*
Yes.

Do I forgive the person/s that abused me?
Yes.

These words were a powerful way to reduce my feelings of injustice and the charge of resentment running through my body. Although my logical mind may not have agreed entirely with the statements, I found my physical body responded strongly and positively to the vibrational charge of these words. This is how powerful our words are. It's a difference you can physically feel. If you stood in front of someone and expressed love, care and adoration for them, the positive vibrational charge within you would be vastly different from the negative energy you would feel expressing hatred and resentment.

In a way, forgiveness prayers allow us to hypnotise ourselves into releasing harboured resentment. Why do we do this? Because our happiness and inner peace are more important.

As I've said before, it's not about crossing an imaginary finish line, it's about reaching a point where we are living authentically in freedom and peace. Our minds can get us part way there, but true healing demands we tune into our bodies and allow them to bring us back to harmony.

The Most Powerful Person Is You

The purpose of healers and helpers is not to fix you, but to remind you of your own capacity and intelligence to heal.

If I can offer you one final thought about embracing your power, it's that many tools, practices, methods and modalities can assist you on this journey to self-healing, but the only one who can bring you to a complete and whole healing is *yourself*. Everything you need to heal your trauma, transform yourself and claim the life you desire is within you. It always has been.

Many people go through life completely unaware they're giving their power away. We hand it to external influences because we don't see that it resides within us. How many of us have questioned our ability to handle our world? Or prayed for someone to come and take our troubles away? What we're saying in these moments is, 'I don't believe I'm strong enough to do this. I need an external force that is more powerful to do it for me.'

Today, all that stops.

We have stepped into our full power now, and it's magnificent to behold. We are not fragile victims. That's just an illusion we bought into. We are whole, we are brave, and we no longer consent to anything that perpetuates the oppressive or controlling feelings of our past.

We are the ones walking on this journey of healing and empowerment, and we've discovered something far more powerful than any of our abusers could ever hope to find.

A complete metamorphosis and awakening to who we truly are.

When we move away from the ego, and the desire to fight, win, seek justice and assign blame, we move towards freedom and love.

When we stop giving our attention and thoughts to the evil acts of the past, we move towards personal forgiveness and trust.

When we forgive ourselves for our role in the events of the past, whether willing or unwilling, we affirm that we deserve to be happy and free.

And when we direct our energy to a life in alignment with the real us, we place ourselves firmly on the path to liberation and true joy.

PART TWO WAVE FIVE

All of this is an attitude, one you can adopt now and carry with you for the rest of your life. When you choose this path, you walk alongside those who are honest, brave and true.

We are the ones who hold love in our hearts. We know that a better life, a freer life awaits.

I encourage and implore you to know, right down to your bones, that you are worthy. You are so much more than your abuse story. You are a shining light in this world. Most of all, you are whole, you are healed, you are loved.

Never give away your power.
Never concede your freedom.
Never doubt your impact on the world.

I hope you're standing in utter amazement at how far you've come.
It's been an honour to walk this path beside you.

Appendix: Healing Modalities

As mentioned throughout the book, I explored a range of modalities and self-care practices in my unwavering commitment to heal from my trauma. I also met individuals who had explored other modalities, also mentioned below, with profound results. From conventional and modern to traditional and holistic, each one supported the self-healing journey. Some you may try only once, and others may become regular fixtures in your weekly, or even daily, routine.

Traditional, Holistic And Alternative Medicine

Acupuncture

A traditional Chinese practice using thin needles on specific points on the body (meridians) to stimulate and balance the flow of energy. Many people experience an emotional release during or after acupuncture.

Breathwork

Conscious and controlled breathing techniques which helped me regulate my nervous system and activate my body's relaxation response. This was helpful when experiencing a panic attack or a release of some kind because it helped ground me in the present reality, rather than anchoring me in the past.

Craniosacral Therapy

A gentle, non-invasive form of bodywork that uses a light touch on the head to improve the flow of cerebrospinal fluid in the central nervous system. Craniosacral therapy can offer a gentle release for physical and emotional stress and enhance the body's natural ability to heal. If you have experienced any form of spiritual abuse, such as ritual abuse, it can significantly assist with reintegration.

Distant / Remote Energy Healing

A practitioner directs and manipulates energy to remove blockages in the body without the need for physical touch. This is a great option for those who have endured intense physical trauma and spiritual abuse.

EMDR

A specialised psychotherapy for PTSD and trauma-related disorders. Eye Movement Desensitization and Reprocessing (EDMR) requires focusing on distressing memories while engaging in rapid eye movements, tapping, or auditory tones. This bilateral stimulation aims to mimic the brain's natural processing during REM sleep, helping to reprocess traumatic memories and reduce their emotional intensity.

APPENDIX: HEALING MODALITIES

Hypnotherapy
Uses guided imagery and relaxation to provide an outlet for emotional release. During hypnosis, the mind is more active and open, which can help shift stuck emotions and feelings relating to pain and trauma.

Journalling
The simple act of writing which gave me a safe space to express my thoughts and emotions and channel my energy. Journalling allowed me to explore my feelings, fears and triggers, and recognise and reflect on them in real time. I found it invaluable in moving through my healing and expressing myself in a safe way.

Kinesiology
The gentle art of muscle monitoring and body mechanics to assess changes in the body. It's based on the principle that the human body already has the answers and kinesiology simply helps communicate to you what your body wants to say. It works to restore imbalances and reduce stress, anxiety, pain and phobias. Kinesiology is also a powerful method of deprograming negative beliefs or mind control.

Meditation
The ability to sit without judgement and notice our thoughts without being pulled into them. This is a wonderful tool to have in your healing toolbox. We all have triggers and distressing thoughts that will emerge, so being able to hold space for them without letting them drag us under is crucial. I found meditation and mindfulness practices incredibly helpful in regulating my emotions.

Progressive Psychologists and Spiritual Mentors
Can act as a catalyst for personal transformation and encourage us on our healing journey. I was fortunate to have access to trusted practitioners who encouraged my growth and healing when times got really tough. They inspired me and reminded me of the power we all hold within us. If you have experienced spiritual trauma from ritual abuse, it is essential to ensure a psychologist has some understanding or experience in this field.

Tapping Therapy
A form of psychological acupressure that combines elements of traditional Chinese acupuncture and modern psychology, also known as Emotional Freedom Technique (EFT). It involves tapping the fingertips on specific meridian points on the body while focusing on emotional issues or traumatic experiences to restore energy and promote emotional healing. EFT is a powerful and fast method to reduce intensified emotions arising in the moment.

Self-Care Practices

I became very intentional about what I consumed while I was going through my healing journey, whether it was food, the content I consumed or the information I absorbed. All of these can have a profound impact on wellbeing, and it's something I'm still very discerning about today.

Affirmations
I integrated many daily affirmations into my routine to short-circuit my negative thoughts and shift them from self-doubt to positivity and self-love.

APPENDIX: HEALING MODALITIES

Dreams

During my healing crisis I started documenting everything I could remember about my dreams. I found recurring themes and messages that directly helped me heal. Decoding dreams is like a training ground for building intuition. The more you practice it, the better you can connect to your inner wisdom.

Food

I made a conscious effort to nourish my body with fresh, organic and nutritious food, and limited junk food wherever possible. I drank good quality, filtered water (no fluoride or chlorine) and learned to listen to when my body wanted to eat.

Fresh Air and Sunshine

I found exposure to natural sunlight always made me more energised and boosted my mood. As well as regulating our circadian rhythms, sunlight triggers the release of serotonin, a neurotransmitter that helps regulate mood and promotes feelings of happiness and well-being.

Music

I became very discerning about the music I was listening to during my healing. I didn't want to listen to violent or low-vibration lyrics, which can be prevalent in modern music. Instead, I sought out instrumental, Eastern and new-age music as it made me feel much 'lighter' energetically and helped raise my vibration.

News, TV and Social Media

Today's news cycle tends to prioritise negativity and sensationalism and the constant bombardment of news can be overwhelming. I made the choice to completely switch off, not only from mainstream media, but mainstream TV as well. To this day, I still don't consume news and I'm very discerning about the movies I watch.

Physical Activity
It goes without saying that physical activity is one of the most important components of a self-care routine. Even a short walk around the block helps elevate your mood and give you an endorphins boost. I found yoga and Pilates to be hugely helpful in rebalancing my physical body after the trauma I'd endured.

Prayer

Prayer is one of the most powerful ways to tap into the infinite power of the universe and raise your vibration. And you don't have to be religious to pray. It can simply be a way of practicing gratitude, bringing comfort and peace and planting seeds of positivity in the world.

These are some of my favourite prayers:

The Ho'ponopono prayer
A beautiful Hawaiian mantra to bring healing and balance through self-love, reconciliation and forgiveness. It roughly translates to 'making things right' or 'moving back into balance'.

I'm sorry
Please forgive me
Thank you
I love you

APPENDIX: HEALING MODALITIES

The Serenity Prayer
A popular prayer to support both release and control.

God, grant me the serenity to accept the things I cannot change,
Courage to change the things I can,
And the wisdom to know the difference.

Metta Prayer of Loving Kindness
The word metta can be translated as 'good will' or 'loving kindness' and helps dial into a positive and loving high vibration. There are many variations of the metta prayer of loving kindness, but one of them is:

May all beings be happy
May all beings be healthy
May all beings be at peace
May I be happy
May I be healthy
May I be at peace
[Repeat]

Howard Wills Transformational Concise Prayer Program
Howard has prayers to bring peace, release judgement, support healing and create abundance in all areas in life.
www.howardwills.com/prayers

Relationships

In the book, I mention the importance of having a trusted support network around you, or even one person in your life who you can be your most authentic, unfiltered and messy self with. This can be a partner, friend, family member, counsellor or psychologist. These people are very special and play an important role in your life because they witness the full spectrum of emotions that pour out of you when healing from deep trauma. Supportive and healthy relationships are a source of comfort, understanding, and validation and these people see you, recognise how brave you are and encourage you to see your own self-worth.

It's important when you are sharing your story that you speak to people who want to elevate you, rather than add to your paranoia or keep you stuck in a trauma cycle. Some people in our lives are used to us playing a certain role, and when we begin to move through the stages of healing, this can be unfamiliar and uncomfortable for them, too. This is where discernment is so crucial.

APPENDIX: HEALING MODALITIES

A Note On Plant Medicines

Enough research is around to prove plant medicines and controlled psychedelics are a valuable tool in healing PTSD and trapped emotions, in particular, psychological conditions that are 'incurable' by modern medicine. When taken in a safe and supervised way, they've been known to help people gain new insights and perspectives on their traumatic experiences and facilitate faster processing and healing than some Western and clinical treatments do.

If you are interested in plant medicines, I encourage you to independently research the benefits of Ayahuasca, Psilocybin (magic mushrooms), therapeutic MDMA and Cannabis/CBD oil. There is evidence and published papers that support the benefit of these substances for survivors of trauma and those with PTSD.

As with everything, discernment is key. Make sure you do your research and choose to work with traditional Shaman's and people of integrity who honour these medicines and the properties they have to share.

To Those Who Helped

I learned that healing was like being in a slipstream. Whilst in there, the right people came at the right time, and I never doubted who was showing up and how. It was an organic and divine-like experience.

Some were healers, teachers or friends, and others were unassuming such as a stranger in the coffee line saying the exact thing I needed to hear in that moment.

This flow-like state existed because I took responsibility and had an irrevocable desire to heal. I held a belief that my healing had no limitation and that I was always going to be sent the exact remedy I needed for where I was in my journey. All I needed to do was to surrender to it, and it *always* worked out for the better.

It is an honour to be able to share the intricacies of my deep and profound metamorphic journey to self-healing. May this book not only be a representation of hope after abuse, but a testament to the communion of the human spirit and our ability to heal and return to love. I am eternally grateful for all who crossed my path.

I promise to continue to live a wonderful, whole and healed life, not only for myself but for the victims of abuse who never made it. Every word I speak today is a word they couldn't. Every day of freedom is a day they never got.

About The Author

SYDEL SIERRA, global speaker, author, founder of the Seeds of Greatness Project is not only a survivor of childhood abuse but a luminary of hope and inspiration. Today, having healed from her lived experience, she guides others on their paths to truth and healing, sparking personal growth and profound transformation.

With over a decade of dedicated self-improvement work, Sydel Sierra has delved deep into the realm of self-discovery. The Seeds of Greatness Project serves as a dynamic platform for a vibrant community seeking to explore a wide spectrum of topics, from enhancing self-worth to reshaping one's relationship with money, breaking free from limiting beliefs, navigating the journey of trauma recovery and more. This initiative is firmly rooted in the principles of self-reflection, individual responsibility, profound introspection and propelling individuals towards discovering their highest path and purpose.

The Seeds Of Greatness Project

To find out more and join a community committed to bettering humanity, offering both in-person events, a blog and livestreams visit www.sogproject.com

www.ingramcontent.com/pod-product-compliance
Lightning Source LLC
Chambersburg PA
CBHW020321010526
44107CB00054B/1922